A VOICE AS OLD AS TIME

CONTEMPLATIONS FOR SPIRITUAL TRANSFORMATION

DAVID BENNETT

FINDHORN PRESS

© David Bennett 2015

The right of David Bennett to be identified as the author
of this work has been asserted by him in accordance
with the Copyright, Designs and Patents Act 1998.

Published in 2015 by Findhorn Press, Scotland

ISBN 978-1-84409-668-8

A CIP record for this title is available from the British Library.

Edited by Michael Hawkins
Cover design by Richard Crookes
Interior design by Damian Keenan
Printed and bound in the USA

Published by
Findhorn Press
117-121 High Street,
Forres IV36 1AB,
Scotland, UK

t +44 (0)1309 690582
f +44 (0)131 777 2711
e info@findhornpress.com
www.findhornpress.com

Contents

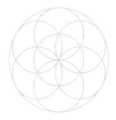

Acknowledgements

Living and writing this book has been a labor of love for a few years and never would have come to fruition without my wife Cindy Griffith-Bennett's encouragement. She was instrumental in writing the proposal and being a sounding board on book style and format.

I would like to thank all my friends and the people who attended my workshops on contemplation and listened to me ramble on about Spirit's messages and the benefits of reflection. I'm so grateful in meeting and getting to know the many new friends on all our travels. The many places we went over the past years led to many inspirational and insightful additions to the book.

A huge respectful thank you to Erin Clermont, my editor, who patiently helped to clarify the sense of Spirit's message over and over. Her helping hand made this work readable.

I wish to acknowledge all the folk at Findhorn Press. Their creative vision from front cover to back, through editing, marketing and distribution, make them the stars they truly are.

Most of all I am deeply grateful to Spirit and our daily communications through contemplation. My connection to my True Nature has grown immensely with your grace, guidance, and love.

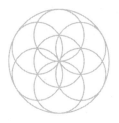

Introduction

Finding a Voice through Contemplation and Reflection

Over thirty years ago I had two near-death experiences, yet they showed me only the potential for living an awakened life. A person cannot change instantly — change requires desire, a desire to develop a new discipline of living. My spiritually transformative experiences did plant a seed of wonder in me, however, which led me on a thirty-year journey toward awakening.

In this book I want to share the reflections and contemplations that were communicated to me by my Soul Family, the beings I met in my near-death experience, to help you on your path toward spiritual maturity. As a new consciousness is beginning to emerge on our planet, people no longer need a traumatic event to shake them awake. Finding a new expanded consciousness is as simple as embracing the awakening process.

It can be difficult living a spiritual life in this world that typically rejects all absolutes. Absolutes like understanding that all things, including humans, are sacred. Many people live life without realizing that deep within the core of our being is a place where our personality and human nature touches the absolute love of Oneness. This place is sometimes called our Divine Essence.

Our Divine Essence draws its energy and power from the universal Oneness, and when our essence feels cut off from the Oneness it withers. When it reconnects, our essence comes alive and we grow spiritually.

It is critical that we acknowledge the importance of inner development in the process of our spiritual growth. Inner development is about finding out who we truly are as we connect to our True Nature.

This pursuit requires engaging in deep Contemplation and meditation. Most spiritual traditions aim for the same goal: reaching a place of Oneness, where we become one with nature, with each other, and with the Divine. But we also recognize ourselves as fallible human beings who live in a world of dualities.

One way to transcend this and reach that place of Oneness, our Divine Essence, is by working with our dualities, our inner light and shadows. Spiritual development inevitably flows in the direction of love and spiritual maturity.

When people turn away from their true nature they thwart their own spiritual development; they no longer move forward. People get stuck because they see implicit boundaries; they see limitations when limitations are not necessarily there; a process that usually begins when we are very young.

The spiritual journey enables the process of spiritual maturity. Our past and feelings of separation can be overcome through a powerful way forward; by the use of reflection. Contemplation allows us to use our inner vision to provide clarity in daily life. We are travelers on the path wherever it leads. The greatest tool you can possess for spiritual development is the ability to be open, accepting, and able to integrate whatever comes through your consciousness, whether it comes from reflective practice like meditation, spontaneously from the Divine, or from dreams, etc.

The more of your True Nature you integrate into your being the greater your spiritual development and expansion of your worldview. Know that there is always a higher wisdom available to guide you to reach your human and spiritual potential.

There is some obscurity during the process of awakening, because we do not know where the universe is taking us. Awakening requires the haziness of not knowing, because everything cannot be solved all at once. We remain in confusion as we slowly let the ego personality fade into acceptance and balance with our divine nature. Trust the process, despite any opposition from others or from your own mind.

Recognize that a fundamental reorganization of your personal identity is not a process to be taken lightly. Such work is long term and may at times require a teacher or guide. *This book is intended to work in tandem with others' teachings.*

As you work toward spiritual maturity in a committed way you will likely have spiritual experiences that will grow in intensity. These experiences are part of your developmental process and are totally natural.

The ideal position of acceptance is to become an empty vessel, ready to receive the divine energy.

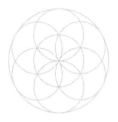

How to Use
This Book

In my daily practice I connect to my Divine Essence and communicate with my Soul Family. I originally met my Soul Family in
two near-death experiences, and that began a lifelong relationship.
The more I worked with my Soul Family the more I realized the
importance of a daily spiritual practice, which provided my path
toward a spiritual awakening.

My daily communications with my Soul Family are in the form
of reflections. Contemplations are a voice as old as time, spoken by
our ancestors and the ancients; reflections still hold the wisdom of
the ages for those ready to listen.

Let's take a moment to define our meaning of "reflection" and
"contemplation" before we move on. Reflections are thoughts, ideas,
or remarks that occur as a result of meditation. They then become
your center of focus in subsequent meditation or a subject for
serious thought or consideration for a period of time in your daily
life. These contemplations provide a path into your divine nature.
Unlike other meditation techniques designed to empty the mind,
reflections intensely focus on an idea while in a state of stillness or
mindfulness.

This book evolved from the daily service of reflections that I
post on my Facebook page, DharmaTalks, and in a blog of the same
name that is available by email. (To find these daily reflections go

.facebook.com/DharmaTalk, www.twitter.com/DharmaTalks
ww.DharmaTalks.com.)

Many times while posting reflections and as I was writing this book, I found that the contemplations and my life criss-crossed in unexpected ways. Like when I'm working with a reflection and I find it is the perfect message for someone who crosses my path in some spontaneous way. Many who follow my daily reflections online report similar experiences.

I've arranged the reflections in this book in a natural progression toward spiritual awakening – from finding and knowing yourself to living in love, and eventually, to finding your purpose. Woven-in are common themes like connecting to your Divine Essence, using loving intentions, and expressing gratitude while on the journey we call life.

I write from the premise of everything being alive with the spiritual energy of Love. Love is the eternal flame that is found everywhere and in every thing. We can all access the wisdom of our true nature so that we can face life's many decisions feeling empowered with clear vision, right action, and a sense of purpose.

It is my wish that this book becomes a tool in your spiritual transformation. Tools such as reflections can assist you in living more purposefully, more authentically, and more joyfully. My purpose in writing this work is not to express any special philosophy or doctrine, but rather to offer bits of truth that might resonate on your passage.

There are many ways to use this book. You can open to any page and see what you find. You might read a whole reflection, or just a portion, and sit with it in your daily practice of meditation. These reflections are meant to stimulate your intellect and intuition and thus open a connection to your authentic self. They may confound, or they may provide "Aha!" moments. You may find you want to work with a reflection for a day, a week, or a month, letting all its nuances and facets bring moments of light into your life.

I suggest looking for synchronistic events that complement the energy of the reflection you are working on. How you engage with the material is personal, and each reader's experience will be unique. Savor each reflection, as if a piece of hard candy were slowly dissolving in your mouth, with many sweet and bittersweet shades.

Sometimes wisdom hits square in the face. As when we walk from darkness into brilliant sunshine and it takes time to adjust. Other times it slowly works its way into our hearts and minds by repeated exposure or over long periods of incubation. In the long run spiritual growth helps unite oneness into all parts of our lives. This is what spiritual transformation is all about.

Reflection practice can be considered a wake-up call that challenges you to look at yourself and the many possibilities before you, so you can change the way you live for the better. Some chapters in this book are significant for growth of your inner life and your interconnection with the Divine Source. Other chapters call to actualize the interdependence you share with one and all. The reflections guide you to know yourself better so you may reach out to others and be of service for the greater whole. It is in service we often find answers to our own spiritual inquiries.

Each of us contains a being that lives forever and a being that will die. Everything must change except the soul. Wouldn't it be unfortunate to spend an entire life without touching your own soul? It is of utmost importance that we do not become so overwhelmed with living in this physical world that we forget to spend time in silence, getting to know the vital life force that makes up our Being that lives forever.

We all have within us an intrinsic wisdom that is linked to the ultimate reality, which tells us that everything is interconnected and we are all One. Reflective work teaches this in the form of hints and suggestions, so as to stimulate your connection to your intrinsic wisdom. It is up to you to realize this wisdom and come to an understanding of how to apply it in your everyday life. In this way you may proceed along your path of spiritual maturity and awakening.

An additional goal is to expand your emotional awareness of the love that exists within you so that you make conscious choices from that love, the very root of your True Nature. In using reflective meditation you will make the connection between Body, Mind, and

Spirit and open yourself to a natural inner harmony, shifting energy from states of uncertainty into natural balance.

Since birth, humanity has had one shared purpose, which is reuniting with the spiritual Source from which we came. We all tread this path in our own way to reach the common goal of reconnection with the Light that shines within us. It is this Light that silently summons us and connects our being to the Source of all things.

Through daily spiritual practice we experience growth and climb the stairway of reunification. No matter where you are on your ascent, you will find these reflections supportive in locating the next step toward nourishing your being. They were created through love and come to you in love.

Today's hyperactive and attention-demanding world makes reflection no easy task. Nonetheless, we strive to find a way to carve out "mental space" so we can think clearly, plan responsibly, and dream effortlessly. From quiet reflection you come to more effective action. An infinite universe of energy surrounds you, and reacts directly to how you express yourself. Your intentions create your thoughts, your words, and your actions. You are what you say, feel, and express. Your mode of expression shapes your reality. Assumptions lead you away from your reality and cut you off from the flow of life. Reflection is the perfect counterbalance to all activities providing you with insight and perception.

At the beginning of each chapter in this book you will see a sacred geometry symbol of overlapping circles known as "The Seed of Life." It has provided deep spiritual meaning and forms of enlightenment to those who have studied it. My Soul Family and I feel this simple symbol provides additional empowering energy to each reflection.

CHAPTER 1

Acceptance

*"Who are you?" Who indeed … I once dreamt I was an Elk
watching the world from the highest hill, overlooking all, with
stamina to outlast time. Then I awoke as me, merely human. Am I
that magnificent Elk or this person? What does an Elk dream of?*

Our ignorance keeps us believing we are absolute. Separate individuals, each independently forging a life with so many other individuals. Am I my job, my family, or a conglomerate of all those personas, which can be put on and taken off as needed? At times I feel like a pillar in the middle of a hurricane, with humanity's madness swirling around me. It is then that I'm quietly reminded by Spirit: "Be the Pillar."

To be the pillar requires a shift, a change in focus, a review of sorts. Try to examine from a greater perspective. Looking for the wonder, the miracle unfolding. It may not be easy, but being the pillar sometimes reveals the clues to finding a direction or future path.

No matter what our life experiences are, or how we feel about ourselves, we are all divine with amazing gifts and abilities to share with the universe. We share the responsibilities of sculpting our souls into loving Light. In the Light we are all the Elk, attentive sentries outlasting time.

Acceptance of the past can free us from it.
Accept yourself to yourself.

As you come to understand your imperfection, you will learn to accept it with the intention of improving yourself. Know this is where we are at this moment and we can step out in the Light of Divine Love where there is no imperfection, there is only simplicity in Being. The freeing quality of acceptance allows us to soar as our True Being.

It can be difficult when seeing yourself clearly for the first time through acceptance, so be gentle with yourself. Know that your True Being cannot be taken away or diminished by others, because your strength lies within it. Continue with this practice until you feel the release of your self-imposed confinement. This may take many days or months, yet developing the practice of acceptance will eventually become a way of being.

Now liberated, flow forward with loving intention and heart-centered actions and life will begin to grow brighter tomorrows. Always know yourself with gratitude and acceptance. This is who you are at this moment, and you are developing this moment with positive intentions.

*Change is the nature of life. Grasping and holding on to
something is not the usual way of nature.*

A covetous nature will distract and knock us off our path. If taken
too far coveting makes us frustrated and miserable. Let Love, with
gratitude and acceptance, show you where you are at this moment.
Focus on what is really important and let the rest go through its
changes. Once that focus is attained a window appears letting in the
Light, illuminating our True Nature. How beautiful…

Trying to become something outside of your loving intention is
a problem. We should let the mud settle and then with a clear mind
use our positive energy to focus on this moment. Allow the future to
unfold and become. Let go of worry, concern, and anxiety. Breathe
in the freedom of this moment.

Life is a rolling wave, ever-moving with incredible force and constantly changing. We all have connection to the universal infinite
living mind. Let it be the rose in our hearts, constantly reminding
us to be mindful, present, and to shine our Light. Positive attitudes
build positive lives and create a more purpose-filled life.

When we expand our idea of who we are and broaden the scope of our awareness, it leads us to challenge other limitations.

The Divine within is ever alert, expanding our awareness so that we see clearly. Expansion creates flashes and peaks of insight linking our conscious with our unconscious.

Stay true to yourself by knowing what is needed and important in your life. Avoid being drawn in by undesired bargains and services you do not need. Instead focus on your unlimited potential, your spiritual connection, and your true daily needs. Stay grounded with a connection to your higher self.

Do not underestimate yourself — put everything you have into this life. The lesson is there with every breath. Every breath holds the possibility for all our futures. Every breath is an opportunity to share and teach. With every breath celebrate the joy of living in this moment of ever-expanding change. We have all the creative power of the universe in our hands, so dare to be all that is within you.

CHAPTER 2

Tolerance

There is no them… There is only we, interconnected and one… We complete each other.

Who is in, who is out, who is included, and who is not… How silly to think this way, to allow ourselves to get swept up in the old customs and social behaviors of "Us" versus "Them."

Drift on the water, carried slowly by a gentle breeze and current, with water lapping the side of the boat. Life's never-ending movement equates to constant change, and the sound of gently lapping water is a reminder. Wander your life with ease, allowing no experience to be excluded or rejected. Continual change is necessary for your movement and flow.

Treasure life to the utmost, but let us not get attached. Let life go through its changes. Allow life to develop its flavor with a curiosity about what's next, all the time supporting each other, following each other, completing each other.

Our feet walk on this earth but our heads look to the heavens.

Some may find it difficult to free themselves because material things bind them. Finding balance can be difficult, but we have a Divine spark within to assist us. If we can be content with this moment and dwell in these circumstances, then we can nurture our spark and let it shine.

Reach out to others. It is surprising how many people are searching in the same way. With this knowledge, determine not to close your eyes before suffering. With compassionate dialogue we find the source of suffering, then with tolerance and loving kindness we build brighter tomorrows.

For years we have been told that we should put away our differences. We instead strive to change this way of thinking and embrace our differences so we may create a more peaceful and verdant world. As you accept who and where you are in this moment, you also accept who and where everyone on this world is in this moment.

Life has a way of mirroring us; we are within each other, and everyone is part of us. Like a flower petal, each of us is a unique segment of the whole, connected, and yet the same as the next petal. When we accept ourselves we can then accept others, becoming whole, carried slowly by a gentle breeze toward empowering change.

As we treat ourselves with gentleness, over and over, we then start treating others with gentleness.

We possess a natural sense of dignity, a sense of Light that touches everything. See the Light in everyone you meet; see the Light in everything around you. We are all bound to a spiritual Oneness. When we understand this, the darkness diminishes and clarity takes its place.

Although we may have benevolent intentions we cannot change people without their consent. Instead, let us attempt to understand others' opinions and knowings, as we come to a mutual respect and common understanding for positive change.

There is always a way to connect to someone, especially when you're no longer looking for "what's in it for me." Enter the stillness within and find that space of pure connection. Open yourself to the higher good in others and you will see all interactions and relations are interconnected and interdependent.

Go within and research your Being, find your essential self.
Find the hidden beauty of mankind.

When you gain knowledge of your essential self then you will know everyone's core nature, free of all singular idiosyncrasies.

You develop compassion for others by a deep knowing of yourself. Once you know yourself to the core, you will understand what is essential and release negative ego. Then the mind can meet itself with understanding. Compassion will flow toward the great adversities that face us.

Forgive all who are lost, those who seek, and moreover, forgive our own missteps. Be free to find higher vision and follow its loving guidance in service to the world. Forever draw upon the spring of flowing patience within: it offers acceptance and assurance with the power to heal. Our silent patience can provide concern and compassion for those in need.

CHAPTER 3

Truth

Release expectation wherever possible — the cover of a book can only show the surface. We do not know the depths until we experience it. Allow yourself to be surprised with the unexpected truth while living in wonder.

We are generally mistaken when we allow our minds to tell us, "I know this, and I know that." Many times we rush passionately forward, not knowing Truth, only to create suffering. After mistakes, we begin to remember not to blast forward without understanding and slowly we change with Love as we seek integrity.

When we speak Truth with all the Love of our Being, others may hear our essence. Words can often be a way to hurt someone, more powerful than a weapon. Avoid speaking thoughtlessly and loosely —gossip and white lies cause suffering. Speak positively of others and raise your healing consciousness. When we speak this way, people feel our Being.

Our honesty, honor, and fairness will lead us to integrity and being whole.

Our hearts crave that we maintain integrity in all that we do. If our life's experiences are built on our truth and virtue then we are living a good life, always moving toward unity with our higher consciousness. The ultimate Truth knows our connection to our Divine Being.

Be true to your higher consciousness through honesty and virtue. We live in a time when extraordinary changes are occurring daily. If we stay within our Truth then we are offering a promise, a beacon of hope, and that is important in these times. Living within our Truth leads to our emotional well-being and healthier living. Let our Truth become an island of calm reflection in these stressful and often chaotic times.

When living within our Truth we take the extra steps to do what is right without sidestepping issues or problems. We do not empower others in life to cheat; we are hurting them and ourselves by not living within Truth. We align with others who are genuine and distance ourselves from those who put on a false face. Our empowered future depends on the choices we make everyday. Our Truth is found in living life and experiencing with clear vision all that is around us in every moment, as well as within. Truth is found when we are ready to learn from beginning to end with understanding and compassion.

When we hear our Truth it resonates in our hearts and points us toward our greater consciousness. When we speak from our Truth our words hang in the air, because our Truth is eternal.

Let the vibration of Truth support and move us closer to understanding our True Being, a dimension of ourselves beyond words, beyond thought. Let us revel in the Truth we find and the songs it creates in our hearts.

Many of us feel the pull toward wholeness. On the road seeking wholeness, we examine our Truth and the need to be fair and equitable in our interactions. We understand that if we do our best, it benefits not just us but the rest of humanity. With loving intention as part of all our interactions, we are contributing to Love that is abundant, and everywhere.

Within us is the capacity of recognizing our Divine Essence and the ability to represent it in a way that allows our Truth to be heard. Empathy helps us feel an inner connection to others, so we might understand how they arrived at their truth even when our truths differ. This helps us to create understanding and tolerance so we may work toward peace within and thereby outward.

Seek the humble loving abode within which the most awesome living power in the universe dwells ... Truth!!

Our Truth cannot be distorted or limited because it is part of the Universal Oneness.

Speak truth upon the winds, allowing it to float in every direction. Participate in the dance of creation without attachment or unreasonable demands upon the world. Live Truth, without expectations or losing oneself in the turmoil of humanity. Become Truth, flowing into eternity with your Being, shining bright certainty.

Breath is life; it is our connection to this physical world. Honor the sky that holds the stars, Grandmother Moon, and the four winds. We have a grand interrelationship with the winds. Breathing in, we bring into our body the air of our environment, absorbing it into our bloodstream and every cell in our body. Our breath mixes with our inner truth and holds us like roots so we may speak our Truth with each exhale back upon the winds. Breathing out we share our essence with the world around us. As we breathe out our Truth can be felt and absorbed by everyone. By sharing it our Truth is known.

CHAPTER 4

Authenticity and Non-Judgment

See what is. See what is not. Follow the true way.

— *BUDDHA*

Let us be Authentic in our lives, unafraid to live with spirituality as our guiding light. Expressing love and receiving love is the only path needed. When we live as Authentic Beings, we experience the brilliance and majesty of life. Being Authentic in life allows us to be brave as well as tender, a different type of strength.

Honesty within yourself and acting in a way that exists within your Truth is your self-truth. If your self-truth is understood, you will no longer judge yourself because you are doing the best you can. Take off the rose-colored glasses and experience the real colors of our world. We are always looking for ways to pad the cold hard surfaces of life so we don't hurt ourselves.

Instead, see those sharp edges clearly. With a consistent discipline, and a solid spiritual practice, you can deal with them.

If something is right in one society, the same thing can be wrong in another society.

Critics and moralists can easily be judgmental of societies they are not a part of. Often when something or someone is viewed as dysfunctional or incomplete they are viewed as different. We tend to create paths and place things on one side or the other of right or wrong, often dividing things into even more categories. Who decided this is that, and that is this?

Nothing is ever complete or imperfect. Our paths only traverse Oneness. In the Light everything is embraced by Love. A person who is aware moves away from judgment, and cultivates non-judgmental consciousness, by simply observing and understanding with love and compassion.

On the path to spiritual maturity we find discernment; an advanced way of sorting things out, it helps us find what gives life a higher meaning. With discernment as part of our intuitive knowing we bring happiness and peace to our circle of family and community. Through discernment we learn to listen within for a way to measure every circumstance, every moment in order to find harmony, forgiveness and compassion. Mindfulness and discernment are our spiritual tools to hear the Divine within and apply it to the sounds of the world.

We are human and living here and now. The Truth for this moment requires we are present neither for nor against.

Life is short but it is full of experiences. We tend to judge those experiences as good or bad. All experiences are opportunities for growth; use discernment to understand which are best not to repeat.

Squeeze all the juice out of every experience so you can learn and develop. When things do not go the way you were aiming, look within and find the strength to examine yourself. Take total responsibility, with no blame or denial. Our higher consciousness will shine a light on the issue and provide clarity with Love.

Let us begin to live today without comparisons or judgments because the struggle between good and evil is the earliest disorder of the mind. Failure and success are just judgments we superimpose on our reality. If we are centered and authentic we have no reason to avoid any experience, and will have no worries about success or failure.

Be open and loving to everything that crosses your path. You will gain a greater understanding and negative ego will fade away.

Truly listening to others who cross your path giving them all your attention during your interactions is strength, not weakness. Our egos want to be right all the time, and often as a result we do not listen to opposing views. Determine to accept differing views through your heart.

Be thankful and always see the importance of loving life. Spend your energy with others who also love life. Release expectations of others, thereby freeing yourself of the frustration of them not living up to your desired results. Forgive yourself for not being perfect and see others as humans doing the best they can.

Happiness comes once we release the grasping and free our hearts of judgments. Happiness and joy are the gleaming reward that's found once you leave the dark cliffs of judgment.

CHAPTER 5

Breaking Free of
Separateness

Stay in your state of peace, inspiration, and refuge. From that place, your voice will be heard by those needing your message.

In these modern times do you sometimes feel your voice is lost in the millions of other voices yearning to be heard? You are never really alone, because you are connected to the powerful Light of Consciousness.

The state of loneliness is far from rare. It is a universal human condition. We learn in meditation about the Oneness we are all a part of, revealing that loneliness is an illusion of the human condition.

Through awareness we help ourselves, and others, to move away from the distractive qualities of loneliness. Many feel disconnected and isolated, yet the pain and disconnection is often from our disconnection with our Divine Source.

Just as there is space inside an atom, there is space within us, the Divine place of peace and love.

If we are concerned with becoming whole in body, mind, and soul, then we are also concerned with the entire world. Are we sharing our healing light with all forms of life on this world? Let us empathically feel the pulsating love in all life that surrounds us. We must no longer isolate ourselves in lonely separation. Instead, unite more fully with all the life in others and in nature.

*We are all in this ocean of consciousness, plunged into isolation
by our own mental trappings.*

Do not be distracted by feelings of isolation. Change your perception by knowing your True Nature, and you will see the vast ocean of consciousness. Just as the bubbling spring is connected to inlets and tributaries on the surface and to the ever-flowing streams underground, you are connected to the ocean.

Don't allow yourself to drift aside, oarless and separate on the surface of life. Wholeness requires us to flow from beneath the surface and add our essence to the Oneness.

Our heartbeat, our life cycle, and our day-to-day existence sometimes distract us by keeping our focus on time and push us toward separateness. Love, Unity, and our True Nature exists outside of time. When we accept this, it becomes the key in the lock that releases us. Life takes on new meaning of everything in this universe, interconnected like threads of a beautiful tapestry.

We nourish our Being with a retreat from the illusion of separateness by returning to stillness. In stillness we touch the love in us that touches the love in others. Do this and weave together in unity, becoming unconditional Love. Just as a water droplet joins another and leaves behind its sense of being a single drop to becoming a flow, unity brings Love.

Separation from our True Nature occurs in the mind. It is an illusion that becomes our reality only if we allow it.

We get lost in our imagined wanderings. Separation from our True Nature leads us into distracting thoughts and being more self-deprecating than we ever need to be. We were introduced to this life as separate and a spectator of ourselves. Life is precious to experience and separateness is a challenge to overcome.

Use your intrinsic skills of understanding and contemplation as interpreters to divine your actions and deeds. As you awaken to your True Nature you can use these skills to live in a manner that is in harmony with your higher self. Focus within on your innermost self until the unseen becomes known and your mind is clear of distracting thoughts.

We all seek a purpose. Yet purpose is not a legacy, unless it is built upon loving intent for all. We have been on a path of separation but now we are in a state of initiation. We are beginning to experience new ways of living in a changing world. Let us re-create our lives — the choices we make now will reverberate for a millennium.

Bring a new sense of Being out of stillness and back into daily life. Look at all the life around you and develop a non-discriminative ability to understand the nature of what you see.

Viewing life non-discriminately, we free ourselves from separateness and see the inter-being of life and nature. Be observant of Mother Earth, use it as a guide: Gaia replenishes and renews herself through the cycle of life. Why do we shut ourselves off from this amazing source of birth, death, and rebirth? Reach out with your energetic roots and branches and connect with Source.

You and I know there is no such thing as death, but is there such a thing as life? Quantum mechanics proves that a non-local part of our existence is just as real as thoughts, feelings, and ideas. It cannot be measured on an instrument. This fact leads us to understand that our consciousness resides outside the physical body, in our higher consciousness.

Our feeling of separateness is a result of our mind grasping and wanting. Our ancestors knew the importance of living in Oneness with all living beings and finding unity.

Are you truly living this life or just playing the dreamer with no particular place to go?

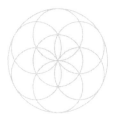

CHAPTER 6

Balanced and Centered

Keep your heart calm and at peace.

We all have responsibilities, but primary is the duty to perform our actions with balance, harmony, and love. Breathe deeply to keep your balance and maintain harmony within. In this way we keep peace and stillness as the most honorable principle in all we do.

When in a calm and peaceful centeredness, we clearly see the importance of every second of life. We perceive others' pain and anguish, knowing how to act with loving intention. Maintaining this sense of existence while we walk this earth can only happen when we are connected to our True Nature.

Within we find peace and compassion for the world. When our connection to our True Nature is healthy, it encourages our higher need for selfless service to humanity. When we are living life in balance, we are gifted with inner peace.

In this physical and spiritual existence we have the presence of all the elements within us.

AIR: independence and awareness of our interconnection, helping spread our message to the world.

FIRE: our Divine spark, giving us a heart-centered focus of loving intention.

WATER: our creativity, which flows into inspiration, stimulating our senses and initiating our connection with our True Nature.

EARTH: stability spreading outward in all directions, giving us a firm foundation to handle any situation.

Let these elements fill our cups, keeping us balanced in all we do. The sense of feeling whole in this human life depends on integrating and balancing these elements into four directions: *Our Thoughts. Our Words. Our Feelings. Our Deeds.*

Create a center foundation of unwavering faith within your Spiritual Being. Allow your True Nature to branch out in these four directions for unity and harmony. Monitor your thoughts, words, feelings, and deeds — always looking for imbalances and blockages.

Our paths are steep, spiraling upward before us, yet with balance and the guidance of our True Nature along the way, we will succeed.

We have all faced long trials in our past or anticipate them in our future. Staying balanced in heart, mind, and Truth are the pillars that will guide us through these trials. We must care for our physical, mental, and spiritual body to maintain balance. When we lose balance we drift away from our center and our ability to be mindful. The further we drift the more energy it takes to return to our center.

Too often we hold on to emotional upsets that hurt us. Often our bodies and the universe are screaming at us to let go. When our blood pressure is high or we are developing ulcers and disease we are damaging ourselves and distancing ourselves from wholeness. We should be letting go of these stressors in our lives. Take a small step in understanding your stressors. With understanding you can find the triggers of stress and forgive or let go.

Examine the nature of disorder within and return to a heart-centered and empathic path, always bringing honorable and ethical energies into play.

Sometimes it can be a moral issue that is causing stress; in those instances it is better to take the high ground and work for change. By putting your energy toward change, you release the stress. Life goes best when you lead from your heart center, in all aspects.

Keeping your center in this fast-paced era is so important — and easier than you know. You have moments to check in and center during your day-time that you normally fill with "thinking." Like waiting in line, traveling in the car/train, time in the shower or the bathroom. Allow a break away from thinking about the mundane and enter the stillness for a more productive day.

Realize that the mind that creates right simultaneously creates wrong. Once we recognize this we begin to find humility. Balance is key: in the material world right and wrong are opposite poles of the same frequency. As we move on our spiritual quest we come to know there is neither right nor wrong — only what is.

CHAPTER 7

Creativity

*It doesn't matter if we do tremendous or small deeds as long as
we do the best we can with what the Universe gave us.*

Our creativity leads us on a path toward our own center of being
– a place where we hear the small, quiet, calm voice that is our
own True Nature, communicating with Oneness. Allow yourself to
become enveloped in your creative endeavors so you may find your
heart-centered Love.

We all have within our being a creative state we can draw on to
lead us to inspiration. This process is very similar to meditation, in
that insights come to us from somewhere beyond ourselves. We all
hold the same power to create from our inspiration. Let us develop
our creativity and recognize we are tapping into the intuitive process.

When we work with any creative endeavor that we enjoy, we
naturally begin to relax. In this relaxed state of being we focus our
awareness on more than just what we are creating. We can use this
time to look at what is going on in our life, to make decisions, and
possibly find solutions to our concerns.

Be aware, open, and receptive to all forms of experience.

The creative process can take us to new levels of experience. Creativity accesses the Divine Love that exists within our higher consciousness. We move beyond the musings of our minds, and connect to the collective psyche of the Universe.

Once exposed to Divine Love, we break through our physical and mental barriers and are forever aware of our greater state of Being and interconnection to all life. With this spiritual connection we begin to fill our actions with loving intention, and thus begin to walk down the path of spiritual maturity. This is true Spirit communication from our Source to our intellect, motivating our ability to act creatively.

Creative spiritual maturity is needed today in our communities, nations, and the world. More and more we need to push open that door to our hearts and minds, to let the Light stream out so that it is visible to everyone. Share your valuable newfound ideas.

Expand them with other creative men and women working for a promising radiant future that is filled with solidarity and peace.

Be like an old gnarled tree, twisting and turning with the winds of opposition. Bend and be flexible with what blows past.

Let no obstacle overcome you. Like an old aikido master, move aside and let momentum do the work. Remember though, an old tree can still provide shade and shelter to those in need.

Still water is so clear and level that carpenters and masons have used it as a measure of what is level for ages. Could we be more like that — level, clear, and reflective without distortion? Can we become a field of awareness flowing gently toward the path of least resistance?

If we rush forward without taking a moment to be centered and present, our outcomes are less than whole. We are like a cloud of probability until we focus on this moment with intention, then things move into alignment. With continued focus we can achieve the outcomes that are more in line with our purpose, which is seeking wholeness.

Acceptance of ourselves, and knowing our Truth are the steadfast tools to reach for to keep us still, and level, balanced, and creative.

Our innermost nature, our true being, recognizes the Divine and stirs from watchful quiet and stillness when experiencing beauty.

Flowers sprouting from the rich soil as if from another dimension create a fellowship through Spirit. Every time we focus on beauty we create more and more windows to the Divine. Return to nature by taking walks as often as possible. Earth, sky, and sea offer their renewing and healing energies for us every moment we connect with them. See the world in a blade of grass or a grain of sand. Escape the confines of technology and reclaim your heart, soaring with the stars.

We are connected to Mother Earth and enjoy and conserve her beauty and healing qualities. All life comes from the Mother and all life returns to her. Appreciate the purpose and power of creation. Be a good steward to her and she will work with you. Feel the life inside and outside your body, feel the life that is present. Keep that feeling of being alive in all you do and allow your presence to touch everything. Bring your focus to this Earth and all that inhabit it, feel the life connection we all share. The expansive awakening we are experiencing is a gateway, allowing us to perceive additional levels of reality.

When we nurture, strengthen, and balance our Being through beauty our hearts are fortified. Beauty, Truth, and Goodness are windows to perceive Oneness. With awareness, we experience spiritual peace, a gift not easily seen, yet deeply felt.

CHAPTER 8

Becoming Aware,
Awareness

Immerse yourself in the unconditional Love and Light, let it permeate your Being so you may carry it with you throughout your days.

Once we have glimpsed awareness and our True Nature, we begin to understand it is not just a notion in our minds. With awareness comes the responsibility to be present, otherwise we move on as if nothing was experienced. If we recognize the significance of awareness, then we understand the importance of opening ourselves to our emerging consciousness and embracing the Light becomes a purpose in life.

We *are* the Light. We *are* awakened consciousness. An essential part of who you are is recognizing your Light and shining it on your unconscious Self. Illuminating the unconscious mind gives you clear insight into your True Nature. This is the path of the integration of Spirit and psyche and becoming one whole Being.

We are participants in all the interactions of our lives. Our intention and actions change everything. Nothing is happening *to* us, everything happens *with* us. We are involved in every breath and heartbeat, keeping our energy level and constant. We do not allow our energy to spike or be erratic. We flow with every situation, taking in and giving back in awareness.

Rise up from the ashes of the past, reborn with Love at your core, and soar with Spirit's freedom to become Awareness and Presence.

Let our consciousness kiss the sky and our Truth be carried by the winds so it may be known. With a balanced connection to pure consciousness let us fulfill our purpose, our destiny to be of service to one and all.

Sharpen your focus; see the details of life all around you. Do not allow yourself to be locked up inside; beam yourself into the world as light does from a window. Listen to what your world sounds like, observe without judging, accept this moment, and move from this moment into the next. Developing focus helps us hear, feel, see, smell, and even taste better.

Having awareness and presence allows us to live in the world, although we perceive the world differently. Living within the interconnected world we begin to recognize the signals our body and environment are broadcasting.

The time has come for us to clear away the film of the unknown from our vision so that we may continue with Awareness and Presence. No matter the course taken, only one destination exists…to find ourselves.

*As we illuminate our path with loving intention, we light the
way for others. Allow the winds of attraction to bring us to
Oneness.*

Isn't it amazing how we are attracted to what we need? So many
of us are drawn toward spiritual development and becoming whole
again in Spirit. Arouse your sense of awareness by focusing on your
breath. Feel the repetitive rhythm of breath, knowing the air you
breathe is the same air all beings in this world breathe. Breath is not
holy or evil: it is just breath.

As you become aware, you humbly come to know that you are
not the body, not the mind. You are simply a watcher, different
from all that surrounds you. The body is your outermost boundary
bound in this density; the mind is inner, with some freedom; the
heart still more inner, touching love. At your innermost core you are
consciousness, pure in your liberation.

We honor the sages old and new. Their teachings are sound. Yet
when looking for a personal connection to consciousness, know that
it cannot be taught, it can only be learned. Study by walking the
path with mindfulness, gaining all you can from daily experiences
and interactions. Do not automatically discard the old because the
new is glossy or elegant — you can still find value in the old ways.

We grow by combining the best of both in our consciousness and
find our way filled with Love and Light.

Move beyond the focus of personal needs. Expand your vision to embrace working with the rest of the world, the whole universe.

At times we feel rooted to the ground and unable to move forward, stuck in our day-to-day existence. Look away from your circumstances, and turn instead to the infinite possibilities in the universe. See a new path with loving intention and break free. Know yourself with total clarity, your strengths, and weaknesses.

When you listen do so with your loving heart and deep understanding. When you speak share your true Being, present your deep Truth. Stand for equality, peace, and a healthy world. Compassion develops when we create openness and gentleness.

To make the present truly come alive, let us open ourselves with awareness.. Expand our consciousness to include the Divine in our daily routine. Ultimately allowing the Sacred Presence to flow into the physical world is a shared human purpose. Within awareness is love, joy, and happiness, a solid footing to build a brighter existence.

CHAPTER 9

Fearlessness

Be quiet, and loving and fearless.

— *B U D D H A*

In this life and past lifetimes we have contributed to creating this world in which we live. Indeed, when we were not living in the moment our actions may have contributed to pain and suffering in the world. As you become aware you see a need for change, and that it is up to each of us to eliminate the unnecessary fear and suffering. To initiate the change we eliminate fear and suffering within ourselves.

Unnecessary anxiety and stress comes when we start worrying about what may come or not come to be. Those fears and concerns become more important than this moment. By focusing all our attention on future potentials we give energy to fear, multiplying the opportunities for fear to manifest. When we stop and realign our focus on the moment we can initiate a future without the need for anxiety and stress. Without thoughts of future failure, if we fall, we fall softly.

Centering ourselves in the present lets our mind release fears of the future and unnecessary suffering. Life will continue on its course, without fear, one moment to the next. Courage is allowing life to unfold fearlessly.

Give thanks amid the change for the opportunity to stay present with Love and Unity.

Welcome change and it will begin right now. Meet change with a welcoming attitude and reduced fear. Look at every change as a new beginning and look for the Truth and Love in every situation. Don't be afraid to jump, prance, or swirl into a daring and beautiful life. We sometimes are hesitant when facing the edge of our comfort zone; stepping beyond ourselves commits us to heart-centered living.

When you are fearless you are not afraid of discovering what reality is and exploring your True Nature. Spiritual maturity means you are capable of dealing with reality. Do not attempt to escape from reality — instead appreciate its deeper meaning. Welcome reality with all of your heart-centered Being, eagerly anticipating what reality will offer and teach next. Releasing fear we flow into our future.

Keep this intention close at hand when starting down the path of reducing fear within:

I am keeping my thoughts positive, without fear, so I may develop my world with my intentions and words. I connect with the vitality of the Universe, I draw upon it, and it draws on me to align support. I am richly blessed.

Be the center of your Being, radiating your good works outward into the world.

The inner life is the true reality; inner guidance makes life in this world more precious and productive. Do not retreat from activity in the world; embrace the ongoing effort of making this moment and your future the best it can be.

The hidden wisdom of the Universe is the knowledge that we are all loved and one with the Divine. When we awaken, this Truth stands out among all else. Our True Nature is waiting patiently for us to clear away the rubble after the high towers of fear and isolation have crumbled, when we will see with clear vision.

Balance your Moon, the woven stories of the mind, with your Sun, the fiery heart. Purify your Being with positive and constructive thoughts, smothering your doubts and fears with Love. Tranquility comes from your heart-centered practice and you will clearly see the wonders of this world.

Shine your Light in stillness to illuminate the path before you.
Shine your Light so those in strife and darkness, fear or grief,
may feel the warmth of Love.

Often people misunderstand how to reduce fears; they think if they have enough power and money there will be nothing to fear. When is enough, enough? The fear remains if now they fear losing what they have. Love is the only way to vanquish fear. In stillness we find a path to our higher consciousness and unconditional Love.

Buddha spoke about not allowing fear in because fear will dull and diminish our ability to love. To reduce fear, slow down and relax, then with the fresh breath of clarity examine the root of your fears. See the weeds of fear and pull them out and release them to your Love. Fearlessness comes from working with a centered heart, so we may jump into life.

Water is a wonderful example of how our Love can overcome obstacles that obstruct our path. We can simply trickle with the least resistant path or we can patiently wait, eventually flowing over and dissolving the obstacle in the flow of Love. Our heart-centered consciousness knows the proper path for overcoming each obstacle with loving intention. Change your life's obstacles, both as participants and observers, with loving intentions.

CHAPTER 10

Joy and Wonder

You stepped on the ground. And the earth, pregnant with joy, gave birth to infinite blossoms. The cheering spread up to the heaven! The moon glanced amazed at the stars.

— *RUMI*

Are we living in harmony with our true nature? Sometimes life can be like a summer craft fair. Some people come to look and wander through the aisles and booths; others come to examine the fine crafts and marvel at their making. Some may be inspired to try to make something new in their lives. Live as a soul in wonder with inspiration in the heart looking to make something new.

Let us remember who we are and our core values, that by nature we are connected to the All and we are one with Love. When we move with joy and Love all can feel it, and when we move with anxiety and fear that too can be felt by all. Let us keep Love within our core and reach out to our brethren who live in fear and suffering. In times of turmoil we should recall our compassion all the more.

Keeping joy and wonder in our hearts and minds can be difficult in our distracting world where so much negative communication bombards us every minute. At times we want to unplug, and that's fine now and then, but we have to live in this world. Just come back to joy as soon as you are pulled away, and before long joy will permeate your mind and heart.

Be inspired to make something new in life, live as a soul in wonder with inspiration in the heart.

Give to life joyfully by sharing your spirit, your life energy. Share the joy and wonder of life that is in your heart with everyone you meet. And always, always, let yourself be happy for others.

Happiness can be elusive. If you are searching for it too hard, you may find yourself always seeking. Our unhappiness masks our well-being and our true nature of happiness. Find the root to sorrow and you can weed out unhappiness. Learning acceptance and tolerance toward yourself is a good place to start. Remember, true happiness and joy originates within and radiates outward, not outward from someone else or other outer schemes.

Happiness and joy are not gained; they are discovered in the core of our being. Many of us have created a wall around our hearts because we were hurt in past experiences. With spiritual maturity the walls dissipate, allowing the heart to recover its independence. One of life's great objectives is to heal our hearts from our own life experience so we can find and experience a broader, more expansive life. Our hearts are stronger than any anxiety or pain, and finding joy in all we do melts away the stress and heals the heart.

Surrender to the greatest emotions of humanity,
wonder and joy.

Joy and wonder lie hidden under the surface most of the time. Look beyond their coverings. Allow wonder to guide you to the hidden joys of life and discover their full spiritual bounty. Observe the glimmer of fascination and foster the childlike wonder and joy that exists within you. Allow it to exist in your being so you are able to explore your world with exhilaration and delight. Within joy and wonder you will find Love.

Magic is in every moment and joy can be found in all living things. Let us find joy and contentment in all we see and do. Our hearts know the rhythm and can feel the flow of joy, so allow your experiences to show you the magic. Our Light sharpens and colors our focus, bringing us a joy that allows us to see the smallest details in everyday life. Don't keep your Light bottled up inside — bring out the joy of a loving heart so everyone in your world may benefit.

When we find delight in every moment, we are being of service to our fellow man. May we always know joy is freedom.

If life is in a state of constant change, then as we live it our opportunities for joy and love must be uncountable, never coming to an end. We can find joy at the start and the end of all things, in a never-ending cycle like a sacred hoop. Try to look for the adventure in life; if we do not seek adventure we are allowing our minds to be only half awakened. Everything in life can show us our way toward living as an authentic being connected to Source. When we find joy it communicates to our pure essence, reminding us we are Love.

Allow the miraculous to return to your life; deliver a fresh bright light to pierce the gray exertion of your mind. With convergence of heart and mind accept a new depth and freshness, experiencing your essential self, interacting with the wonder of your daily life without words, judgments, or labels.

Slowly disentangle the old patterns ingrained in your intellect, return to your dawn of being. Your sense of wonder will lead you to inspiration and to your higher consciousness.

The possibility of delight and freshness is always there. Catch it, and enter into that first stage of wakefulness. This phenomenal world presents you with the possibilities of freedom to follow your joy and wonder. Stay connected to your heart and flow from it, then let go, and jump into life with a true spirit of gratitude and thanksgiving.

CHAPTER 11

Inspiration

Clouds come floating into my life, no longer to carry rain or usher storm, but to add color to my sunset sky.

— *RABINDRANATH TAGORE*

Do not look only to the sky or mountains for inspiration. Look beneath the trees and shrubs. Our greatest inspirations can be at our feet. Look closely, for it can be the smallest thing, a leaf, or a bud, to imbue the greatest love and grace. Nature provides quiet reflective places to listen to your inner voice. Look deeply into simple natural events — sunlight on the wet grass, or a leaf floating in a stream. While reflecting, Nature will tell you about your life journey.

In all stages of life we are connected with inspirations that teach us and remind us who we are. This year and past years' held reminders for each of us, reminding us of our paths. In moments of stillness we can each reflect on our Divine role by connecting to our Love. Through clear vision we can walk from the fog into the Light.

Become an explorer of your deep inner potential. Voyage through the stillness of the heart and mind discovering the power of Love.

The untapped potential of our inner space reveals inspirational resources undreamt of ... an inner peace and purpose.

We all have something we love to do that brings about inspiration, whether it is music, art, crafts, writing, or whatever pleases you. As you do this activity that brings joy, devote all your attention to it and see what new ideas pop into your consciousness. Explore these new ideas further by trying to accomplish some of them. While working in creativity hearts sing when new inspiring ideas are heard above the chatter in our minds. In this subtle way Spirit communicates with us.

Our ideals are our greatest inspiration, lifting us to do wondrous things that are desperately needed. Living in inspiration when partnered with loving intention and action is the solution to many difficulties. Lift your hand to others so they feel your inspiration energizing their hearts.

Your personal mission in this life can be known. When you choose to find your peaceful presence within, that is the time to ask yourself the question. When we are present we see the flow of mysterious coincidences that guide us.

With awareness in tune we find clues to our purpose in our daydreams, dreams, and intuitive knowings. Strive to listen to the wisdom of someone that delivers synchronism, because these moments are indicators of our purpose. We must be the spiritual detectives of our own lives, always available to the hints that present themselves.

Miracles are available and happen every day, especially when we are open to them.

Our path in this life is to seek inspiration for others and ourselves. We learn from our past experiences because they give us clues to the present, and tell us how we can allow the future to unfold. As we travel our life's path with our hearts centered, our focus moves away from ourselves and we see the beauty all around us. Once we center and get out of the way our Divine Being connects with us instantly. We perceive obstacles in our path with clear vision and observe the grandeur all around us as we find the way through.

We all step out on our own individual paths, many times in the dark and feeling alone. Yes, we have our individual pathways, but with the awakening of more people around the globe we find that our inspirational paths that used to run parallel are now crisscrossing. Shine your inner Light of inspiration so others may see your path is close to theirs.

We are interconnected and interdependent on one another to make this world a better, more inspiring place.

Which is more conscious, the butterfly, or the flower? We are all doing the best we can with what we have been given, whether we stretch our wings or stay rooted and firm with the earth and elements. We are meant to be living in an awakened state of consciousness, in harmony with our physical surroundings.

This state of Being sparks our creativity and fills us with inspired insight. In this state we remember our innate mission, and we recognize others in whom we see ourselves.

Throughout history humankind has been struggling to live spiritually while on this earth. At this moment we have all been called here and we all have a Divine mission. We are working together to raise our consciousness so we might hold those spiritual values in our Being at all times.

In order to accomplish this, be at peace, listen to the divinity within your heart, and know you can accomplish your facet of this spiritual tapestry. We are not alone, knowing as we work together we are weaving a brighter inspired vision of tomorrow.

CHAPTER 12

Guidance and Paths

On the path of Love we are neither masters nor the owners of
our lives. We are only a brush in the hand of the Master Painter.

— *RUMI*

Life is an adventure. Life is unpredictable, going from the known to the unknown. Climbing peaks that have not been climbed, moving into uncharted seas with no chart, only your inner guidance to lead you. The only way to become a master of yourself is to go into the unknown, unafraid, despite fear, and develop your spiritual guidance. Salute the Divinity within — for which there is no adversary to distract you.

The spiritual path gently balances wisdom and heart-centered peace and neither judges nor harms. The spiritual path flows through life's distractions maintaining harmony. No one is better suited to recognize your path than you, so follow your inner expert. In stillness you already know the answer to every personal challenge.

Give your mind permission to hear your awakened heart. Build your strength and sensitivity in the solitude of stillness, so the pain of the world does not wear you down. Be the strength and sensitivity of loving intention when there seems to be none. Be the comfort of Light when others see only darkness.

We have within a hidden teacher with unlimited patience, acceptance, and knowledge. We have only to unlock the door we hid him/her behind.

Divine guidance has already laid the foundation and is waiting for your participation. Open the door to it and listen to have Spirit available and at hand.

Once freed, allow Spirit to persuade you to try new things, adding new experiences to your life. Stretch yourself to be open to new possibilities and witness the potential of your Being. Intuitive knowing, Inspiration, and Spirit do exactly what they are supposed to do: Guide.

Thinking through a situation is helpful, but feeling your way with your heart is more encompassing, bringing together what you know in your mind with knowings beyond your physical self. Contemplation of the Divine within can transform any situation with heart-centered understanding.

The resolve of Spirit is as great as Light, showering us in Love equal to nothing here on earth.

Our True Nature knows and understands it is up to each of us to recall and reestablish Love and Compassion in our daily practice. Our intuition is always broadcasting, and we only need seek with our natural curiosity to fire up our intuitive receptors. Break away from the routine and hunt for answers. Ready your primeval intuitive nature to receive messages from our interconnected world.

Around every twist and turn of your path, you will find Spirit patiently waiting to assist and give guidance. Spirit is not there to carry your burdens, but to show you the outlets you have to lessen the load.

Guiding us without imposing, Spirit instills in us a sense of wonder and awe as our purpose is revealed. Keep an eye out for your dharma — your purpose — in every aspect of life and find your Divine self smiling back at you.

Intuition is a part of us; it is the connection to our higher consciousness shining down upon us from Oneness. To receive the answers we have only to accept the communication and ask the questions. The soulful path lies in following Spirit's guidance. It is easily recognized by its joyous, nurturing, and loving nature, as in this affirmation:

I rest satisfied with Divine administration, for who am I to say, "I know the big picture." I am free for all things to come to pass with gratitude for my connection to the Divine.

When we feel we are aimlessly adrift, we need a direction. Converge mind and heart through contemplation and daily practice.

Truth knocks on our door all the time, but do we open ourselves to it? When we hear our Being speaking deep in our hearts we know and understand Truth. Yet do we cross the threshold and live a life of loving intention, a life of meaning? Spiritual insights are a part of us, like each breath we take or each beat of our hearts.

Our Truth knows no boundaries, no limitations; spiritual insights are timeless treasures we find on our path, steadfast mountain peaks in the sun's golden rays.

Your path flows like water: allow it to buoy you up and support you. If you try to swim in a different direction the flow will make it difficult. Why do we work against ourselves? Forgive, release, and allow. Trust the guidance the Universe sends: be in the flow instead of working against the tide.

Enjoy and trust your True Nature by diving deep, swimming far, and navigating with the flow, allowing it to propel you forward. The more time spent in the flow the more natural and effortless life becomes.

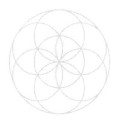

CHAPTER 13

Heart-Mind Relationship

You come from the celestial spheres but seduced by this clay form you believe you belong to the earth. Why have you forsaken that which is your essence?

— *RUMI*

Are your thoughts directing you, or are you directing your thoughts? Are you being dominated by your thoughts? If you are present, allowing your nature to be as it is, then thoughts do not consume you. Instead thoughts inspire and fascinate; we are not hooked into ambition, instead we are *allowing*. We live with less push and more give.

When your mind is clear, each thought is transitory. When there is a feeling of discord in your mind you work toward noticing and examining it. If there is disorganization in your mind, the world seems disorganized. The same with drama, if there is drama in the mind, the world seems drama-filled. The mind is drawn toward disorganization and drama. Spend a few minutes each day to clear your mind and break the connection to disharmony.

By placing awareness and Love on internal conflict the discord will unravel. Maintain harmony and balance in the mind so the heart can shine through. With a clear mind you can see the reality and beauty of the world through your heart.

Free your thinking so you may feel your heart intuitively and know with new vision how magnificent and fulfilled life can be.

Let go of the way things are in life, so clear vision may reveal how it can become reality. Understand the complex web of how things are to have a positive empowering effect to improve the world. Thinking is not bad, especially when it is in partnership with your heart and soul. It is then we become aware of the sacredness of the Universe.

The mind when aligned with the heart unites with universal loving intentions. As soon as you start participating in this harmony, you become realigned with the wholeness of life. A much greater spiritual dimension exists within us in the Light of Oneness.

Do not hang your identity on your thoughts; instead expand who you are by identifying with your True Nature. That interconnected part of you reaches out to the Universe of all Beings, united, with unlimited potential.

The mind visualizes time, and articulates futures and pasts
until it gets bound in its own complicated trap.

Future, Past, and Present can be a mind game, but don't let it be. Time is only one dimension of our reality; focusing on time traps us in that curious linear element and allows the ego to brew past and present worries into a negative spiral, dragging us down. Live in the world, but not through the wanderings of the mind.

Don't let the past or the future stand between you and this moment. Our minds love to drag us into past memories or projected fantasies and desires of the future. Stay attuned to the present; never miss the opportunity that exists for you this very moment. Stay living in the present, mindful of the mind's wanderings and allow life to unfold.

Be part of the present, infusing positive energy into exactly what is called for in this moment.

Wouldn't it be nice to have clear space in your mind where you could consciously expand your awakening? Reducing compulsive and unconscious naming and comparing of everything we perceive can achieve that clear space. Every time we like or dislike we limit our possibilities, limit our thoughts, and imprison our possibilities; our ability to create a future stagnates.

The first step in clearing the mind is to observe the moment without interpreting or classifying it. Allow the moment to *be*, accepting it as it is. Work with what you have available toward a better future keeping the love in your heart in center focus. With less clutter in the mind and heart we have more clear space, and more room for positive prospects.

The clock starts ticking when a thought is beginning. Be in love with what is, whatever it is, or whatever direction it takes. We hold the threshold of the future in this moment and we have a lot to balance in this world. Don't *think* past or future, simply *be*. Time would not exist, if it were not for thought.

CHAPTER 14

Integrity

*Music propels my heart toward an open connection of myself.
Already moved to tears of joy and love. Fingers touching strings,
all that is ever needed is within the moment. All that is ever
needed is within.*

When we live with integrity we do the right thing without try-ing. Integrity is the state of Being that comes when we are in unity with our True Nature. We act with no ulterior motives and want only to be honest and true to our wholeness. Many times in life we ruminate over and ponder issues that cross our paths. Some-times our culture may ask us to compromise, but how many conces-sions can we make before we lose ourselves?

Here is one solution: *You can think about it with your head, but navigate it by your heart.* In that way, you keep your heart and mind in balance while maintaining your integrity.

Integrity is beautiful to the discerning eye, because its simplic-ity shines a direct course. It does no good trying to figure out the right action intellectually, because we recognize the genuine from within. Our Being is benevolent, allowing us to move ahead freely without the need to "think about what's right." Just as a bird doesn't go to class to learn how to sing, we already know what is appropriate because right action flows naturally.

When we speak from our Integrity our words hang and resonate in the air, because our Integrity is eternal.

When we function as whole beings, according to our True Nature, we develop our personal integrity and virtue. Through integrity and virtue we find the greatest joy and wisdom. Our integrity holds healing tears of joy and love, recognized by all hearts.

Open your eyes to integrity. Many times it comes dressed in different garments or is heard from unexpected sources. We must absorb integrity into our Being, allowing it to sink to our core so we understand ourselves.

We are small on our path of Truth, yet part of something greater. As we develop self-confidence and understanding of the positive elements within, we begin to see the pattern of relative truth, which is part of the greater Absolute. Our integrity cannot be distorted or limited because it is part of the Universal Oneness.

As a plant needs the sun, earth, and water to grow, we need balance in all elements to quiet and focus our internal energies. In this way we are amenable to know the universal truth of Love.

Developing a strong disciplined mind that is balanced with the heart opens the portal to awakening and wholeness. Our minds tend to wander, moving us away from our heart center. So let us move our hearts closer to union with our minds.

All physical life has a rhythm and flow, and now it is time to add a new pulse of spiritual consciousness. It is time for us to swing from the intellect toward a greater connection with a spiritual focus. We have beaten the drum of reason for too long. Do not abandon your passion for developing your intellect, instead build upon what you have and merge the study with your spiritual focus for even greater understanding.

The new rhythms are more intricate and, entangled with a back-beat and syncopation, create beautiful flows of intuitive growth, inner peace, Presence, Gratitude, and Love.

Integrity breathes peace into turmoil from the heart, forgiving and letting go.

If you are upset then your mind is in turmoil and in control. You cannot be effective in helping others or yourself in that state of mind. Do not leave problems unresolved because it will leave you unbalanced. The longer you take to resolve turmoil and return to balance, the harder it will be to recall the initial root of the problem and weed it out.

If you lose track and become overrun with weeds, you can always reconnect in stillness and let your Light shine through so brightly that it vanquishes from heart and mind all the monsters of desire, envy, maliciousness, and greed, returning you to integrity. Let your heart and mind be filled with tranquility, Acceptance, Tolerance, Truth, and above all Love.

All problems yield to a focused heart and mind. Although we cannot will the mind alone into focus week after week, a heart-centered connection to it taps into the universal consciousness that supports our focus. Love and beauty make the work of overcoming problems relaxed and cheerful.

Understanding the physical and mental layers of life comes from a mind that works in concert with Divine Unity. Let us move beyond the physical and mental levels, reaching the heart and eventually the soul level.

When we tap into our True Nature's potential we increase our energy and begin experiencing transformation. We cut through our incomprehension, awakening our heart and mind to greater under-standing and integrity.

CHAPTER 15

Enlightenment

It is said that God's Light comes from six directions. From where? asks the crowd, turning left and right. If only you could look neither way for a moment.

— *RUMI*

When we look deeply into ourselves to see our misjudged steps in life it can be painful. It is easy for our egos to see other people as foolish, but finding our own foolishness is a great step toward wisdom. Knowing your inner being and True Nature transforms your consciousness and brings enlightenment.

As you begin to transform, others may not understand the change in you and your world. These misunderstandings can cause great suffering and bruised egos, so use mindful love and compassion to see the circumstances clearly. Always remember to be gentle and love yourself, and everyone else, because we are all connected to the same Divine Source.

At times of great suffering the ego is diminished, and in extreme cases it may collapse, allowing your True Being to emerge from the entanglement with your physical self. Understand then that your higher consciousness is your true identity, expansive and without boundaries of matter. Now you come to understand the harmony of the Divine.

Breaking the illusion of separateness allows the beauty of Love to move us and know our potential.

Even in the early stages of enlightenment we recognize the amazing gifts we have to share. We expand the ways we express love, creating positive change within us and within our circle and communities. Within each and every one of us exists the glory of enlightenment.

Even more exciting is that our potential is encoded in our DNA and our Being has complete access to it. In stillness we peek into our True Nature and know that we are all so very much alike and separated only by our minds.

Individual enlightenment is a deep spiritual experience in which you see your own Nature and then must adapt to live a dual existence, in the physical world of Self, and one of universal consciousness.

As more individuals find enlightenment they will come together and create new communities based on mutual acceptance, respect, truth, and loving-kindness. The enlightened are like the pillars of an ancient temple, standing on a firm foundation of love, reaching upward to hold in place the protective cover of peace and harmony.

Each of us individual pillars, strong and holding up our own weight, all the while contributing to the whole with our amazing gifts and strengths.

*Become flexible to new ways of Being that emanate from the
heart, truly giving love unselfishly to benefit humanity with
your compassionate actions.*

To find enlightenment we need to awaken from our stream of never-ending and compulsive thinking. We will experience the release of our mental grasping when we commit to an ongoing attempt of letting go. If there is no inner recognition of our spiritual self, however slight or momentary, then we are missing the touch of greater awareness.

Once kissed with our own spiritual potential it draws us inward, where our heart is awaiting patiently to merge with our Divine Nature. Awaken to the Divine within, to flow with life, releasing the rigid grasping of past, present, and future. Develop receptivity to higher consciousness and allow it to guide in quiet times.

Continue to learn not to force the future into the present; instead allow the present to flow naturally with loving awakened consciousness. The spiritual self with its extrasensory perception and awakening capacities is the root to acknowledging our Spiritual Being.

May we stop procrastinating and put our spiritual houses in order, so that we may climb out of this box and begin to live a whole life of enlightenment. It is your birthright to live as a heart-centered person connected to your Spiritual Being.

Carefully study your inner relationship with the outer world.
See how your inner states are projected onto the screen of life.

We learn how to live in harmony with the rising and falling energies of our lives. We flow with the ups, downs, ins, and outs to progress toward our goal of spiritual enlightenment.

Do each thing in its own time, and nothing else. Stay in the flow and rhythm of life, one step at a time, and one breath at a time. Be aware of life's rhythms: Are you in an expansion phase, when your life energy is building, or are you in a reduction phase, when it is dispersing? We find spiritual advancement by using the right action for each phase.

All of us on the spiritual journey are actively seeking the Divine. But we should also know that the Divine is seeking us. We are aware that Oneness has planted a flower of loving kindness in our being. We understand that we are not alone, that there is always compassionate Light piercing the darkness.

The Divine swirls all around and within us; it is up to us to recognize this and step into the vortex. Spin with the Divine, let spirituality unfold into growth and enlightenment. Open the eyes of your heart and mind to see clearly.

CHAPTER 16

Being

There at the center of our Being, a light eternally burns. Our body is fast asleep but our light is alert, and awake. We are asleep even while we are awake, the light is awake even as we sleep.

Let us all gain the center-point of our Being so we radiate our Light and Love in all directions. Once this point is located we can respond infinitely to what is and what is not. Generate clarity for what is truly important, leave behind the drama, and step forward with renewed purpose. It is no longer about having; instead it becomes more about *being*.

Let go of everything, if only for a few minutes a day. We find our harmony by letting go of the stress, the needs, and above all the fear. Then we move forward with confident presence.

In these hectic times, as the world is rushing around us, stay true to Being. Don't allow yourself to be swallowed up by the incompatibility and conflicts of the day. Stay true to your wholeness of Being. Use the harmony within to brighten your heart with Light. We are dancers in an age of complexity in which we are expanding and ever-changing.

Whirl with Truth always in our minds, light in our eyes, and fire in our hearts. Step forward in the present, increasing your resonance, racing onward toward awakening. Appreciate the experience of Being.

Once we have crossed the bridge of seeking Oneness we understand that Being is the deeper Truth.

Honor perceptions and feelings as they come and go. Follow the path as it unfolds and brings you closer to awakening. It is so important we find a way to live, and become a realization of our own personal Light. There is no more important purpose that needs fulfilling, so become a beacon, become a sign, shining your transparent luminescence in service to humanity.

Open your heart and allow the Light of Being to fill you. Feel your shimmering essence expand to touch everyone you meet. Be true to yourself: do not let the chaos of our world influence your Being.

With presence, shine your Light with Truth, thus empowering the moment. Turn your perception around; look at your Being from all directions. Experience pure love and compassion for all life. Awakening begins with knowing ourselves and accepting our Being.

Use the Spirit of the Universe to refresh your Being from time to time, and recharge your creativity for living life. Draw in Universal Love to your physical heart and mind to infuse every cell in your body. When we care for ourselves we care for all of humanity, strengthening the world.

Allow a focused zone of Being, with ever-expanding boundaries, to percolate into a new authentic you.

When working on developing ourselves we sometimes come to a limit of our understanding, and we become confused. We can either step back or push forward. Moving forward from our empathic center allows us to find solid footing once again and emerge from the fog with new understanding.

None of us are the same or perfect. We are all living our lives in this imperfect world making mistakes, yet we are working as best we can to live our lives fully. Our mistakes can be painful, but through the pain there is always a window that opens onto greater wisdom and insight. Even in darkness know always how much you are loved, and carry that Love in your heart.

In physical life we experience everything as having a duality; everything has its pair of opposites. Opposite poles are really only two extremes of the same thing, with varying degrees between them. In the Light everything is complete and a part of the whole, Oneness existing in multiple dimensions.

Emergence of our Being lies in our realization of the Divine Presence in our neighbors, in our antagonists, and in all life. Release the notion that there is only one way to awakening. Exclusivism divides us, so we must dissolve concepts of privilege in order to liberate ourselves to Being.

The central innermost part of our vital essence is Light, which is harmonized with Love, full of joy and mingling with all of Creation.

On this beautiful and wondrous day, and every day, emphasize the need for creating a silent space within. We open ourselves with innocence, curiosity, and awe, as we begin our day with an intention to be focused with clarity and in communication with existence. We choose stillness so we may create a spacious gap within, empty of the idea of "I" or "me."

Our own noise is like a wall encircling us, separating us from our Being. Contemplation allows us to break free of that noise. In order to find your Being you must first be sincere and willing. Growth comes rapidly once you reach willingness, because as inner resistance melts away, you open yourself to participation.

Within stillness is an empty room filled with Light. Reaching it requires emptying our cognitive faculties. As we look into that chamber of light we realize it is our Divine Nature. Dwell in your chamber so you may see clearly.

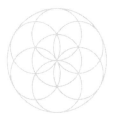

CHAPTER 17

Untapped Potentials

Locate your essence, your consciousness, which is always present in the clamor of life.

When we find ourselves in unfamiliar territory from time to time, in those moments sense your Being. Do not lose yourselves in the noise of the moment. Take a moment to unplug from all the technology and visual sensations and focus instead on *Being*. When we tap back into the world around us, we can then see it as it really is, multiple streams of consciousness of a single wholeness with infinite potentials.

Keep in touch with your primitive instinctual side. It warns you when trouble is in the air. This innate knowing, which happens minutes, hours, or even days before your world begins to shake, is a natural part of Being, and when balanced with your heart can keep you and your community safe.

Often it feels as if our whole Being — animal, intellectual and Spirit — is looking outward and embroiled in needing control. Examine all aspects within to conjoin the shadow of your animal, instinctual side, with your intellectual mind and strengthen your connection to the Divine. Then all the potentials of the universe are in divine alignment.

Allow your Being to soar on the currents, like a balloon
reaching new heights where you can see clearly in all directions.

We all have within us the potential to rise above our physical circumstance. Like the example of a seedling overcoming the force of gravity to break through the surface and strengthen in a new dawn. No matter how hurt or wounded we may be, no matter how weak or hardened, we can recover.

Our Being has the potential to beckon from the Universe all that will strengthen, nurture, and protect us. The universe has a rapport with our needs and recognizes what is similar, and develops a kinship with our Being.

Relax into the happenings of life, and know that all of life's experiences are manifestations of vibration and energy. Tune in to your Being and experience yourself as an exquisite expression of nature wherein all potentials exist. Be willing to take a chance and plumb the depths of your Being — until you examine those depths you may never know the vast untapped potentials of your whole Being.

Our relationship with the Divine and ourselves is what ultimately gives us life, and when we look into the depths of our Being we become One.

Dance with the Light of Being; know your potential is moving toward wholeness. We all desire to be whole and yet in this human existence we live with the duality of Self and Spirit. Bringing them together in balance and harmony to realize your True Being is found through your inner space. Stillness brings us to our inner space where we discover empty spaces in our thinking, and there in those spaces our True Being patiently waits for our discovery of us.

We understand that the core of our Being is Love and Truth, which are inseparable from who we are. Love and Truth connects us to our Light. Yet we may spend lifetimes concealing that Light. Love and Truth are just below the surface of our consciousness seeking to break free and shine brightly for all to see. Occasionally we glimpse the magnitude of our Being, love directed by love — that is, love expressed unconditionally.

A glimpse into ourselves calls us to discipline our thoughts toward more loving thoughts and actions. Love has the power to transform us into living expressions of our unlimited Being.

By facing our harsh realities and knowing our magnificent pleasure we find the truth in Being.

We hear it all the time: "Why bother…." We have the potential to learn and practice Love and Truth. Proudly reveal with Love and gratitude the authenticity of who you are. If you play a character beyond your true self you do yourself no good and neglect your True Being.

Become a watcher of your life so it may allow you to love unconditionally, without the attachment of drama and ego-based events. See with your inner eye, ensure that whatever happens remains untouched by attachment and drama. Yes, unhappiness is there inside you, but also happiness — they are together, if you are present.

As we observe ourselves we recognize the Divine Being in others, an interconnection that brings them more into our clear vision. The more we connect this way the more we produce a greater return to consciousness for all of us.

Unconditional consciousness is not absorbed in or distracted by thinking, instead Being is felt as expansive and unconditional.

CHAPTER 18

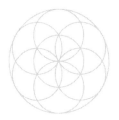

Awakening

We are adolescents at the beginning of a shift toward awakened maturity. In this transitional stage of physical and mental human development, each of us will cultivate the emergence of awakening within ourselves.

Imagine a time of awakening, in which Truth, respect, honesty, and love are the rule. We naturally do what is right and balanced without the need to think about it. We simply flow with universal consciousness. We are on the cusp of the time of awakening, with more and more of us connecting to our Being and starting the transformation of consciousness process.

Appreciate this new way of living; blossom in all aspects of life. When we can open our hearts, becoming strong and deeply loving, our consciousness expands. Since the beginning of time humankind has been in the process of returning to our source of Being. Gradual at first and increasing with each era, think of us as a great river flowing to the sea, picking up increasing speed and volume with each gained tributary, expanding eternally toward Oneness. Things are moving so fast now we feel like we are in a free fall into the future.

At this moment our consciousness is speeding toward the mysterious energy of life, part of the shimmering river that carries us onward. As we move forward, we begin to awaken to our connection to a reality within us that transcends limited everyday existence. Our inner consciousness is being brought to our outer consciousness.

Become the essence of each life's interaction; become the practice of Truth and Love, making it a seamless and graceful partnership with our higher consciousness.

As human beings, awakening is our inherent nature, not a cultural phenomenon. Take what you have learned, your insights and direct experiences, and give them form. Become the embodiment of your awakening process. Put out the call to awaken from your physical slumber to a new reality of expanded spiritual consciousness.

Arouse the connection between yourself and the unified consciousness of your True Nature. Lift yourself from the denseness and reach out to the Light. Spiritual endurance and resilience are necessary for those on the path toward awakening. Live with the Divine Essence of your True Nature, and persevere through difficult moments and challenges that might tempt you to compromise your vision and values.

Now is a time for growth and the opportunity to open to new understanding and clarity. We are naturally good, and to know that within us we only need to look past our mental grasping. If we live in the roots of the tree we will never climb to the tips of the branches and connection to the greater world that waits. When we release our grasping of things, when care and proper nutrition is given to our body, when we focus our vision and find harmony in the moment — then awakening will find us. When we unify our knowledge and heart, Spirit finds a fertile field to dwell, sprout, and grow.

We are watchers, all different yet all connected to everything that surrounds us.

Awakening the connection to your inner consciousness creates awareness, a fire that burns away negative ego, greed, possessiveness, and jealousy. All the while awareness is enhancing all that is beautiful within: positive ego, grace, and Divine Light. As we become awakened, we become witnesses. We come to understand that we are not our body, mind, or even our heart. Our body is only the house we live in. At our innermost core we are pure consciousness, a part of Oneness.

May there be swiftness to our Awakening. To bring forth awakening we need to cultivate a seed of self-knowledge. Then we must look closely at what is sprouting. Our objective in awakening is illuminating our being with the Light of Oneness.

Develop awareness of the simultaneous rhythm of the universe and the rhythm of your heart. Feel your heart as one with wind and wave and the leaves falling to the earth. There are a multitude of latent qualities within each of us. It is time we begin to explore, recognize, test, and interact with those qualities. So as we push toward more complex shifts in consciousness we bloom instead of becoming distracted.

When we dream that we are dreaming, are we about to awaken? This life is a dream of sorts, and when we reconnect to the Oneness the delusion is clear.

Everything comes and goes; our physical existence is always changing, always in flux. Awakened consciousness is the only constant; we must strive to attain it for the freedom it brings.

Awakened consciousness is our goal and our gift. Those on the path find contentment in their work and lives. They are reducing their needs and wants. The more they fill their cup with Spirit the more they can give to others.

You can find them with a glint in their eye, smiles on their lips, and you can feel their penetrating look into your core. They are everywhere. On the path to awakening no one else can tell you where your path leads: only you can discover you. As you search deeply within, you will find there is always more to fathom. Others may journey with you, but they cannot go within you, or awaken you.

Contemplation is an excellent tool for strengthening the heart. Look back periodically and review where you have come from, what obstacles you have overcome, and how much you have increased your spiritual strength. Touch the past with compassion and love and let it be instructional, but leave it in the past. Do not long for the "old days," which saps your strength for this moment and suppresses the momentum to move forward in awakening. Allow your inner-child to birth innovative dreams into this world. Help bring humanity to new heights of awareness.

CHAPTER 19

Consciousness

The soul of man is immortal and imperishable.

— PLATO

Earth represents the energy of life and primordial creation, from which all things are born and to which all will eventually return. Our consciousness merely visits the physical energy of Earth and then returns to the Oneness as a drop in the ocean of Light. There are two forms of consciousness: inner consciousness and universal consciousness.

Inner, or individual, consciousness is a spark of Light that is part of the greater universal consciousness. You, the individual, contributes to the whole as the universal contributes to the individual. Together they form Light, which is the Love that makes up everyone and everything.

The fastest thing in the universe is not physical light, as in the scientific definition, it is universal consciousness, which can move from place to place instantly and be in multiple locations at the same time.

Love is the action and motivator that interconnects us, so that all of our consciousness can be One. Our Higher Consciousness does not need to penetrate anywhere. It is already here, within everyone and everything. We only have to allow ourselves to be aware, and then the doorway of consciousness will open.

Consciousness is timeless. We need only to step outside ourselves to glimpse the vast expansiveness.

From our DNA to the farthest galaxy, consciousness is the organizing principle in the emergence of form. Once we connect we become a sentient participant. Consciousness flows through us into the physical world all the time, yet it increases exponentially as we become aware. It flows into our thoughts and actions to guide and empower us with acceptance, tolerance, truth, and Love. With mindfulness we resonate with these vibrations as we strive to reduce suffering and create harmony.

As a new consciousness emerges on the planet, we no longer need a traumatic event to shake us awake. It is as simple as voluntarily embracing the awakening process through stillness, Being, or releasing form.

Surrendering to a new dimension of consciousness allows us to blossom with compassion and love. *Being,* in alignment with unconditional consciousness, leads us toward wholeness. Our distinctive character is a flash of colored light on the grand tapestry of Divine Unity. Each of us contributes to the flow, so let us upload our reflection for the greater good with this intention:

I will dwell in a place where my nature can bloom, a place where we honor the flowering of consciousness. I will bring the Divine from within into everything I do and everywhere I go. I will see you and your Divine Nature and honor the blossoms in your garden, for we are together in this journey of life.

When we agreed to incarnate in this physical form we brought a sliver of our Light with us, and in that way we are always connected to our essence.

We cannot misplace our consciousness, because it is our essence. We are a part of it and it is a part of us. Just below the surface, within us, that connection to Universal Consciousness can be found. We can touch and hear Spirit, be in touch with our personal truths, and know the wisdom and feel the rhythm of the Universe. Once connected to our inner consciousness we link to feelings of overwhelming calmness, and breathe deeply with Oneness.

When still and centered we become so much more than our physical body and mind; we bring in our higher consciousness, allowing a greater expansiveness. We become who we really are: consciousness, unconditional and eternal. Once the door to your inner consciousness is opened, positive inspiration will begin to flow. Move with this creative energy and bring it into all aspects of life. Bring fresh excitement and joy into what you do and thus into the world.

Our concepts of what is possible and how we see reality affect how we live, and affects the energetic flow toward our potential futures. Our co-creative energies are influenced by the complex interactions between thought, knowing, and our True Nature. Our health, our lives, our community, our world are all dependent on our expanding consciousness.

Feel the loving warmth of heart-centered living.

We are multifaceted beings with unbelievable stores of strength and fortitude. Yet we are also fallible humans. Living within this duality, we seek to be whole. The two strands of consciousness are intertwined, like the structure of DNA.

Weave them together in serenity, returning to wholeness. When we embrace Love, Compassion, and Unity we strengthen those habits in our consciousness. When we give in to anger, lust, or greed we strengthen these negative habits in our consciousness. As we introduce and repeat positive habits those habits will be near the surface of our consciousness. When we quiet a poor habit it sinks away from the surface, and eventually the scars from poor habits will fade. It is our goal to rise above the surface.

When we let go in stillness we quickly experience our connection to Universal Consciousness. Once there we can accomplish spiritual growth, send healing to others, and develop channels to our higher consciousness to use in our daily lives. As we enter silence the silence becomes us, warm with love. As we join our consciousness with the Universe, the expansiveness of the Universe becomes us. We become nothing, so we may become everything: all Love, all Compassion, within and without.

Experience limitlessness as you expand your consciousness throughout the Universe. With limitless intentions we feel our infinite potentials becoming our heart-centered experience.

CHAPTER 20

Meditation / Stillness

I stood at the edge of the canyon and heard an endless wind
blow. It blew off into silence, endless silence, endless Love.

As we connect to our essence, through stillness we find wisdom. We gain freedom, knowing there is no limitation either in time or space. Facing reality directly and encountering it face-to-face liberates us. We take the interval to look into reality silently, without thought, which can be a hindrance or barrier. Meditation is seeing what is and seeing what is not.

Exceptional learning happens in contemplation. We can read and quote sacred writings from memory, but true learning comes from finding Truth for ourselves. It is only by experiencing Truth on our own that freedom happens. The nature of stillness is loving-kindness with wisdom that is recalled from our Being. When it is found within then it is recognized as your True Nature, genuine, with no model or set rules.

Wisdom is self-generating, spontaneous, and free, only wanting to express itself. It acts with integrity, whole and undivided. Socrates said, "Look within, Know thyself," but he didn't give us a method. The journey to stillness is private, that's what makes meditation so powerful. Stillness allows us to break through our separateness and know our True Nature.

Through stillness your heart will find its way home, to the nature of Oneness.

"Simplify, simplify," said Thoreau. If we clear our minds we will see how truly simple life is. Stand in the river of silence; wade in up to your chin. Be aware of every ripple and all the powerful currents. Let the currents pull you along in a constant stream of knowing. Awaken with the flow of consciousness thrumming in your veins.

Meditation is like swimming in your own infinite ocean of energy, your Being. You have heard the song resonating within and remember the harmony of the path inward. It has the natural flow of familiarity. Let us flow on the path toward Oneness, toward wholeness.

Using stillness keeps your mind serene like the stillness of a lake. Let go of assumptions about the world and use the lucidity of your mind to see clearly, unperturbed by distractions. If a wind of disturbance ripples the surface of your serenity go deeper into the stillness. Your practice will make this a walking state of being.

Listen deeply to the rhythm of your heartbeat and breathing; notice how the whole body relaxes with deep listening. It causes cooperation between our conscious mind and our higher self. The more we practice deep listening, the further inward we go toward stillness.

Tune in to the universe until it feels like one thing. Find the stillness that pervades the world of nature.

In the quiet of the early dawn or the deep hours of dusk become aware of the stillness without thought. Connect to the formless and timeless dimension within. Become one with your true essence, your Divine nature.

Prepare with breath by inviting the wind into your lungs and be your friend to carry your message forward. With feet on the ground connect to every cell and invite your energy to flow like the water in a gentle yet unstoppable force. Touch your heart and let the fire of love wrap you in its warm embrace. Stillness is diving deeper within and soaring upward into your sacred place where you experience the expansion of unity with consciousness. Step forward on this earth while being present and build tomorrow.

The essential nature of humanity is a coming together in a more authentic way of inner stillness, peace, and wisdom. Trust your inner wisdom and continue changing the way you live to be more centered and noncompetitive as you connect with wholeness. As we reach toward Oneness, we change. Our way of living changes as we evolve into heart-centered beings with loving intentions toward our entire earth family.

In the dynamic peace of stillness, the light of our True Being permeates all of us with inspiration and resounds with strengthening Love.

As we begin the process of change it will be carried in our Being forever. We are learning to heal the fissures of *dis*-ease and becoming whole. We allow the boundless calm of stillness to flow throughout our life until there is no distinction between our physical world and our awakened Being. We see the reflection of our Light in both.

Ask that the selfless aspects of your nature grow into balance, so that self-absorption and self-gratification are reduced. Sit for increased mindful connection to your True Essence and Divine nature. Balance your ego with all aspects of your human nature. In stillness breathe into your heart a breath of unity with your higher nature. Discover your mind in tune with the mind of the Universe. In this expanded and unified consciousness allow your heart and mind to focus all that you know yourself to be. Recognize: I AM Present, I AM Being, I AM Love, I AM.

Exploration in stillness illuminates the knowing that we are holding the co-creative Source within. We find there are no boundaries for the potentials of our Divine energy; all unfolds so we may see the Divine within. Offer up a call to your Divine nature for guidance and inspiration. Then begin working on today's project, knowing that Spirit is with us, helping us hit our stride. Allow guidance and inspiration to flow.

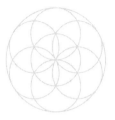

CHAPTER 21

Harmony

With an eye made quiet by the power of harmony, and the deep power of joy, we see into the life of things.

— *WILLIAM WORDSWORTH*

Your own harmony, joy, and health can be a great source of nourishment for others starving for spiritual food. Flow with your inner knowing in your exceptional moments of harmony, sowing positive seeds of empowerment and awakening. Change in yourself is changing the world, for you are the most beautiful Being, living a purpose-filled life. Keep moving forward without fear, and find outcomes brimming with courage.

When we allow our heart to connect to our higher consciousness we breathe a sense of harmony and peace into the world. We have an awareness of the calming nature that heart rhythm brings. It pulses meaning to the depths and ripples substance on the surface of any situation. Enthusiastically share this harmony.

Experiencing the harmony within allows us to experience the harmony of the world around us. We are on the threshold of a momentous time when more and more people are embracing the path to awakening and living with purpose. This bursts with potential to relieve suffering and help others to have more fulfilling lives.

Unroll beliefs down to our core being, and examine them. There you will find the root of our Being is Love.

Harmonize with the love at your core, allowing it to cultivate your thoughts and actions in loving focus, so you may once again become whole. Speak positively, hopefully, thankfully, and above all with a core of love. Allow your words of love to heal and create seeds of positive action. Release any disorders by refusing to give them any thought or energy — in that way we speak in harmony. We also recognize that our spoken words resonate in our Being, leaving a lasting impression.

Happiness is simple, after all; we need only to keep harmony within our Being. Our Divine Nature contains a purity of spirit that is part of the greater Oneness. Instead of looking outward for happiness look within to know your Divine Nature, where harmony and happiness reside.

When in harmony with the Universe, we see the beauty that is all around us.

Do you pay attention to the air your breathe? Only when breath is labored do we naturally notice. This is an imbalance — it should be the other way around. Do you perceive your True Nature; or are you unconcerned, like with your breath? We are all perfect, wise, and virtuous if we allow ourselves to open to our True Nature. When you feel that you exist in the world as whole, beautiful, and in harmony, it resonates throughout the universe, adding and contributing to the positive nature of humanity. We all benefit when we feel this vibration, and it quickens our way. The Universe then sighs a warm smile of contentment.

Do not allow life's adversity to spiral into greater suffering. Infuse love into every situation, and ask your higher guidance for harmony. Listen to the flow all around you: it is like hearing music that rhythmically flows in time with our breath. Move into the flow and watch as harmony washes adversity away. The continuous cycle of giving and receiving creates a vibration that reverberates to restore balance and unity, which gives us harmony.

When we find ourselves in a time of imbalance, let us begin to sing an old song that has always existed but is all but forgotten, a song of harmony.

Adaptability is necessary to cope with unexpected disturbances in our environment. With it we can correct imbalance and return to harmony.

Taking time to understand the situation we are in goes far in realizing new empowering outcomes. Take care when admiring the natural beauty of this world with all the wonderful creatures that abound. Our society's tendency to exploit natural beauty ultimately destroys or defaces it. Seek harmony with our world, give back as well as take, and future generations will be grateful.

Our Earth, Gaia, is an intelligent presence of self-preservation that is composed of all living beings, rivers, mountains, fire, and air. We all share a common goal to protect her and to walk upon her with respect. Allow yourself to touch Gaia and feel her loving embrace.

Let us study nature as a practice in harmony, as we establish harmony within ourselves. Everyone possesses well-being, wisdom, and goodness. We all have the ability to sing and weep, exposing our Light within. We all wish to be free to give and receive love, and grow on our life's path. Many times we get caught hanging on to the past or worrying about the future and that keeps us from moving forward.

We are all from the Oneness and all we need do is ask Spirit for help. Help release us from the distractions. Help us find the harmony that resides in our nature, and allow our life to unfold with heart-centered action.

CHAPTER 22

Peace

Tranquility
Let us find peace in our hearts.
Let us nurture peace in our hearts.
Let us be humbled by the power of peace in our hearts.
Let us speak with peace in our hearts.
Let us act with peace in our hearts.
Let us promote peace in all hearts.

A re you worried about the world? If so then visualize a world at peace with all its peoples experiencing a conscious awakening. Let us tend to our own garden spiritually and physically. In this way we will inspire through our example, a quiet emergence. Peace begins within, so cultivate a loving heart so that you walk a path of peace and love. With each step we are one step closer to world peace. Just as Gandhi said, *"Be the change you want to see in the world."*

We need a totally different world, where hate is not taught. Look at the contradictory messages in our world. We talk about peace as we prepare for and support war. We talk about brotherhood as we disrespect others. Are we listening to our Truth? Are we at peace with ourselves, only needing what is present? If so, we should always be available to Truth. Live in this world with a connection to a greater Oneness. Live with your Truth, watching and moving in the world as it endlessly changes.

Foster your Peace so it expands and branches outward, reaching beyond your dreams into a bouquet of accord.

Commit to helping our world become a more peaceful and compassionate place. As we commit ourselves we become a flower of hope, unfolding with beauty and grace. Find the calm peace within your stillness; bring it into your day where it can grow.

Touch the Love that resides in your heart and find forgiveness. While living this life forgiveness is one of the most liberating experiences. Forgiveness releases resentment, hatred, and anger, planting the seeds of peace to grow a stronger tree of life. Make peace with this present moment and feel all the Love that is available to you.

Look out for our home, Mother Earth, by returning balance to nature instead of destroying our own habitat. Build our communities with sustainability in mind. As we awaken so will our natural desire to bring harmony to our lifestyle and Earth. We must not turn away from problems; we must create new stability in our culture.

Finding Peace within, that is being Present.
Helping our fellow citizens, that is being Present.
Living with heart-centered consciousness, that is being Present.
Being and sharing, that awakens Peace and Joy.

In our life we come across folk who are upset and vent their frustrations at us. The last thing they need is someone yelling back at them, feeding the frustration. What is needed is Peace, so accept that the person is hurting. Eventually they will feel the peace and begin to change. Be an example of peace and show others that anger and frustration can be worked out.

Peace is the first seed of change. We have within all the ingredients to turn our existence into Peace. We are all interconnected, contributing to a collective consciousness. As groups focus on violent and disrespectful trends it affects us all. As groups focus on peace and harmonious trends it affects us all. Our internal peace allows us to view situations without judging and work in the moment with what is present. Peace within allows us to live in the universe as an indivisible whole, without fragmentation, in a place where isolation does not exist. Peace begins within. Now is the time to be present with peace.

A great challenge for all awakening beings is to focus on respect for one another and no longer view others as separate. Stop thinking of everybody as individuals or groups. Start acknowledging we are a global family capable of giving love and receiving love. Love starts at home, and now is the time to act.

Extend your Light to your brothers and sisters with the breath of love and compassion.

Allow your Light to mingle and circulate into a healing force that extends to our world. With cooperation we can affect a peaceful re-design to the world's malfunctioning systems. A sense of Peace flows through and with higher consciousness. Peace comes to us when we recognize our oneness of spirit, our oneness with the universe, our oneness with love, our Oneness. As we surge with the Oneness we become aware it is the natural bridge of our Being, and we glide over to it.

When we have a deep spiritual experience we are touched by Peace, which leaves us with a calm mind, a gentle heart, and hum-bled spirit. Inner peace develops when we bring our spiritual experi-ences into our daily lives. We learn to go on and on listening, learn-ing, and yearning for peace. On our path we each cultivate a peaceful state… a peace that is simplicity, a peace that is pure energy, a peace that is Love.

CHAPTER 23

Living in the Moment

Sleep my friend, but if you do the Light of Truth will slip by you unnoticed. Asleep in the darkness of the night you will miss the splendor of the day.

— *RUMI*

In youth we thrust ourselves into the thick of life and all it has to offer. Why do we slow down as we age? Instead, let us experience all we can throughout life and squeeze all the juice from existence, because living fully brings a wealth of new comprehension. Dance the dance and enjoy the moment. Live in the moment enjoying whatever is available, drinking in each moment.

If you love what you are doing now, act as if this is going to be the last moment. If you hesitate, your mind will give you suggestions, "Do this or do that." The mind can go on and on postponing things, and before you know it opportunity has passed by. Do good immediately. Why wait? Do good because it directly brings joy to your Being and to the world at large.

Do not waste a single moment, put all your energy into this moment. Happiness is always found in the moment that is now, here right now. Do not allow yourself to be trapped in the past or future. We have so much potential in this moment. What is time, anyway, but the progression of moments? If we fill each moment with gratitude, respect, and Love, we will see our efforts returned in kind.

Our dreams are outside of time; they do not know past, present, or future. But dreams are an indicator of our present Being. Dream your future now awakening.

Be completely at home in this vast universe; be present, manifesting your core qualities. Be conversant, peaceful, and healing toward all. Do not get trapped in the search for purpose, because this moment and the next are part of your purpose. Your future is rooted in loving actions that stem from this present moment.

Link to the universal creative power within and feel its expansive wave encompass your Being. Enjoy this precious moment, and the next, moving with the flow of each moment. Do not wait for change, swirl into your redefined future. Make today fresh and a new start of moving forward. Leave the past behind because those old patterns are over. If you wait and wait for your life to be different, you will only find yourself waiting. It takes action to change this moment and the next. Pursue your vision of excellence in whatever you do.

Remember, though, that rest and activity together are the steps toward living in this moment and bringing our dreams into fruition, so always do both.

Openly question every moment of life. Remember that one decision can change your entire reality.

What is your relationship with this present moment? Is this moment a friend or a foe, are you in control or are you allowing the moment to unfold? Your answers are related to your potentials. Are you choosing to work with your individual spark of divinity, using all that you are to be present?

Do you feel the connection and love of Divine Energy? A steadfast call from your Divine Essence is singing to you through your heart to melt your insecurity and weakness. It buoys you up in times of challenge and stress. It feeds your awakening soul and encourages you to continue moving on your path. Take a moment each day, each hour, to connect and fill your cups so you may be fully present.

Each morning breeze reminds us to breathe deeply of this moment, establishing our consciousness into our heart-centered being. Move with the flow of the breeze throughout the day. Stay aware of your breath; notice how it feels to take in a breath and the feeling of letting breath out. One or two conscious breaths helps keep you centered and mindful of the moment. Take note of your breath many times during the day, and notice what is going on around you, as an observer without judgments.

When we become Present and full of Love for ourselves, that is the moment we become successful.

We are all born with seeds of potential, and all we have to do is make the short journey of inches (metres) from our head to our heart and allow these seeds to join forces. There may be noise and chaos in our environment, yet within there is only stillness and peace. Every challenge can be overcome when focus is entirely in this moment.

We are at a crossroads, and it is time to stand tall and shine across turbulent waters. Create a path of Light that transforms chaos and restlessness into peace and respect. The shimmering Being within is a rhythmic signal broadcasting peace, love, and cooperation. It reminds us to bring loving attention to all our activities. Our Being fills the atmosphere and can be felt by all that are in tune. Even those who may not recognize it are aware there is something special here. Choose in every moment who you are and what you wish to experience. Even in the darkest moments you can choose to shine your tranquil inner Light, giving hope and promise.

When we live in this moment we become aware of our connection to one another. Whenever meeting someone new, give your fullest attention and open yourself to see the Divine Being within that person. This builds the unifying field of awareness among us all. Discover that the moment you are in is unique and fresh, never to repeat itself. This moment is absolute Love, which puts warmth in your heart and a smile on your face.

CHAPTER 24

Presence

Belong to the Wind in the Trees, Belong to the Clouds in the Sky
Belong to the Waves in the Seas, Belong to the Green Grass of Earth
Belong to the Stones under Foot, Belong to the Heat of the Flame
Belong to the Steel from the Forge, Belong to the Vastness of Space
Belong to the Stillness Within, Belong to the Present.

How do we use our past experiences, and how are those experiences going to help us deal with the present? Heart-centered change starts within each of us, and if it cannot be done within us it cannot be done in collective communities or nations. We know change can come into being by lovingly examining our past experiences, which gives us a glimpse into the rhythm of our purpose. Let us change the way we think. Move away from the belief that we are conditioned by the past and turn instead to this moment. Focus on the present with gratitude and with positive intentions. Know that our experiences have shaped us and given us tools for the present.

Some of us pile one moment upon another throughout life, totally forgetting ourselves. By living in the moment, allowing each element in life to come to pass, we are seeking harmony of the whole. Oh, that it would be that we all find peace in the present and sing as a bird upon the dawn, flying forward with virtue. Be present in the world and watch it change, fluctuating moment to moment, letting the future unfold like fluttering wings of a butterfly. Enjoy the change, the newness, and all the surprises it brings.

If we are reactive we become entangled in form, however, if we allow all the possibilities to shine and follow the empowering path we foster our Being.

How are we treating this present moment — with love, with respect? Or are we calculating how we will benefit from it? Do we hate where we are? Are we addicted to reaction and feeding our ego, or are we calmly nourishing our Being? How we treat this very moment affects our future. We can initiate moving in a positive and unshackled direction by being Present.

Life can be like a freeway. What is behind you is past. What is ahead is new, exciting. But we need to be present, in the moment, so we can navigate the curves and interchange. Too much looking backward in the rear view mirror or into the future will run you off the current road you are on. We are more productive and spiritually healthy when we eliminate the preoccupation with past and future.

Time is linear and only one dimension of our vast reality. Focus on time traps us in that singular element and allows our egos to brew up past and present worries and doubts, which leads to anxiety, creating a negative spiral reducing our vibration. Allow this moment to be as it is, and dissolve the confines of time.

No longer grasp and hold on to the unnecessary.
Become transparent and focus on love.

Release this moment, trying to drag it into the future; a new day looms with limitless potential. We tend to carry our burdens, grasping them, carrying them from the past into the present. This entangles us in resistance, which binds us to ego. Allow your Being to shine through difficulties and complicated circumstances, finding clear solutions. Fill your heart with deep love, strengthening your peace so you may move forward unencumbered. Success in life is being present in life *now*. That makes the future easier, because you allow it to unfold. Strive to bequeath nothing and let go of the notion of legacy.

Trying to change the past or worrying about the future is like focusing all your energy on a narrow portal of nonexistence. The past and future do not exist except in your mind. The only thing we control is this moment, along with our intention for the future. Make your intention positive and do not hide from life; participate even if you work behind the scenes to create positive change.

So many people drift through life using only a small part of their potential. Do not allow the winds of fate to blow you away from the present moment. *Be* here to the fullest, and enjoy the blessings of life with your crystal clear loving-intentions.

Some there are that torment themselves afresh with the memory
of what is past; others, again, afflict themselves with the
apprehension of things to come; and very ridiculously both —
for the one does not now concern us, and the other not yet…
One should count each day as a separate life.

— *SENECA*

Spiritual growth requires us to be persistent. It's not just a passing fad. A daily practice of being present with a focus on mindfulness of the moment is a wonderful starting point. Spirituality is connected with the present and if we live outside the present we may miss the potential of the here and now. Once we begin to recognize the flow of consciousness that is Presence we begin to understand that we must not row against the current, nor is it good enough to simply float with the current.

A more desirable action would be to direct our will along the current, aiding the experiences of our lives. Move with the flow, the ebbs and tides to which we attach our intentions. Our future is not fixed; the future is only an array of possibilities.

The future weighs upon the present, reminding us to complete each step in our life experience so it unfolds in a deep and natural rhythm. Always keep the basics close at hand: stay relaxed, focused, and mindful. Set your intention and release it, allowing it to unfold in whatever way is beneficial for all, in the same way that you lovingly created it. Our life experiences build layers upon layers, to become who we are in this present moment. Our layers guide us toward who we will become sometime in the future. Let us lay down foundational layers of peace and love throughout our Being.

Spirit Communication

*Make friends with the angels, who though invisible are always
with you. Often invoke them, constantly praise them, and make
good use of their help and assistance in all your temporal and
spiritual affairs.*

— *SAINT FRANCIS DE SALES*

We are all citizens of this world with the ability to speak directly with our higher self. Once we comprehend our being human and connection with our Light we begin to see the kinship with all things that are born and grow upon Earth. Spirit speaks to us in so many ways — from nature, an unknown person, or from a son or daughter. A message or knowing appears to us at the right time and place. Our interconnection allows the communication to come from all sources. Allow yourself to be connected.

Our connection to Spirit should be considered more precious than all other possessions. We care for our spiritual relationship through stillness and allowing our mind to quiet enough to listen. Our personal method to connect to Spirit can be learned or found through self-discovery and, if maintained, becomes our state of Being.

Spirit is a part of the Oneness within us. In contemplation we hold truth and love as we seek to be more aware in every moment of our day, Spirit then finds expression through us, helping us toward awakening, so we may create peace and compassion in all we do.

Walk in step with Spirit and find Love, Joy, Peace, Forgiveness, and Selfless Service.

Spirit is in all of us, patiently waiting for us to put aside our ego mind so we may step out with Spirit in this turbulent world. Spirit's voice whispers, showing us a new day is dawning in which wisdom, peace and love is ours. We are here to help those who cannot hear and live without guidance. Share the scent of Spirit's roses effortlessly upon the breeze so all may enjoy. We may never be in this moment again, so let us be present.

When Spirit calls, listen and lovingly fulfill the call. In our busy lives we tend not to listen, or worse, put the call on hold. When we do not heed Spirit's advice we later see the missed opportunity and many times regret it.

Spirit never appears with demeaning, biased, or negative character. Spirit's touch is loving and empowering, in our best interest, facilitating healing, and growth.

Our spoken words have energy, our thoughts imbued with love have the capacity to set ripples of energy in motion.

Whenever you are setting an intention, place love in the center and ask to receive the best for all involved from the Universe. Perpetuate the energy by giving yourself to it and returning to your higher self. When touching that higher consciousness we find our home, our core, and we bring that central part of our being into this life. A great sense of healing and becoming whole comes from the creative potential of words and feeling the flow of energy from the Divine. Let us help one another by speaking and interacting with heart-centered connection to Spirit.

To have the best connection to our spiritual communication we benefit by keeping our energy clean. Energetic hygiene is best achieved when we focus on higher vibrational states like Love, compassion, and service to others. Allow lower, grasping energetic states like envy, greed, and lust to dissipate. Be aware of your energy and the power it holds. Keep yourself calm and full of gentleness. There will always be a challenge or struggle, yet if we maintain a quiet strength we can scale the heights of higher good. Hold your compass of Love true. Steer through any turmoil, always able to come back on course.

On the way toward spiritual maturity you form a union with your Divine Essence, weaving together a relationship based on Love and mindfulness. Each communication that occurs between you and your essence is sacred.

We all have an inner voice that speaks to us with the ultimate wisdom of the universe. Give yourself time and space to listen. It is the voice of all that is; a divine presence within each of us gently guiding us toward what is best. Explore the actions that will call up your Spirit communication. Explore the actions through your higher connection and listen for the message.

Deep Connection, and collaboration with Spirit bring peace and unity. Take time to notice the peace that comes from Spirit communication. Use words to bring your feelings to the surface, so they may ripple outward with loving intention. Through sharing your visions, ideas, and perceptions from contemplation and Spirit, we become comfortable being in a state of connection.

Become open to the world and Spirit, it speaks to us all the time, we only need to be open to understand. Once we receive the message we have a responsibility to be of service.

CHAPTER 26

Energetic Exchange

A flower is very much like our life, it mirrors us in budding, blossoming and gradual withering. We see the short duration of our lives here on earth compared to eternity. Let us not wait to blossom and share our loving intentions with the rest of the world.

In the Light we see the interconnection between all things in our universe. Every time we have an interaction with someone an energetic exchange takes place. In physical life we barely notice this exchange unless we train ourselves to be sensitive to it. For example, every time we judge someone it creates an energetic exchange that is disruptive, blinding us to the True Nature of the situation or person. Use clear vision and loving intention in all interactions.

What energy are you sending out? The Universe will respond and return the same vibration back to you. When we live in such a way as to be of service and supportive, then we receive support from the Universe. Love must be put into action, because we live in a dynamic universe of energy. Within us we have the capability to sense sacred energy. If we focus our attention we can project our sacred energy in a desired direction, influencing other energy systems, thereby exponentially increasing sacred energy and contributing to the Divine Light. Let us focus on expanding our resonance of Love.

Exchange between the world and us is constant. We are forever growing from integrating the many new parts of the emerging new me/us/we.

With every interaction of our lives we give a little bit of ourselves, and receive in return a small part of the persons, places and things with which we interact. At times we may feel conflicted but Divine Unity holds us in harmony until we seek within for our True Being. Whenever we think of others or speak with others we exchange energy. Thus we are always growing as a person. We would all do better if we no longer spoke ill of others or gossiped. Instead, help one another overcome obstacles and heal the earth.

We cannot find ourselves in all the events that pass by in a day, a week, or a lifetime, but we can glimpse ourselves in the relationship between things. As we constantly exchange our energy with the Universe, it connects and binds us to oneness. We give energy and receive energy with every movement and breath. Cultivate loving intentions so these energetic exchanges resonate with your Divine Essence. Keeping stillness in your heart and mind allows you to recognize your energy as it passes to and fro. We can see this demonstrated in nature's clear, unbiased exchanges of energy teaching us unconditional Love.

Every positive touch we make with one another works toward the greater good. Be like the worker bee, mindfully gathering pollen from each flower, fully engaged in the task at hand, cross-pollinating with love as he flies.

Don't keep it all bottled up inside, breathe in and breathe out. Understand that everyone is breathing in and breathing out. One breath has so much to say — do not keep it locked up. Find beauty everywhere; even in birth and decay the cycle is unbroken. In one breath, let out the Light and see the shimmering effects. Keep the cycle going... peace, tranquility, and bliss. Shanti Hum — Sanskrit (I am peace).

Breathe in a calm centering energy into your heart and achieve harmony. Do this while drinking some cool clear water or while walking. Release any painful emotions and find peace. The whole world is our palette, move with your body, your mind not thinking. Follow the flow of the vast Universe, gliding through empty space until nothing remains but pure joy and Love. Be present with each breath and become one with everyone. When we move this way our energetic colors spread like rainbows.

Energetic threads bind us all together.

We have within us the capacity to feel the emotional vibrations of others. This can be confusing, so take time to understand when you are feeling someone else's vibrations and not your own. Everyone's emotions vibrate at the same frequency, and when we are in the vicinity of someone experiencing specific emotion it strikes the same vibrational chord within us. When you are emotionally close with someone, you can tune in to his or her emotions no matter how far the physical distance between you.

In stillness our breath becomes a rhythmic current of energy that flows through us, connecting us. Bring this unlimited energy to your dawning day as you focus on the great tasks that you can now accomplish. Breathe new life into every day. Send out loving thoughts with every breath during your practice. Direct the tremendous power of your breath to carry blessings and inspiration to those close to you. In that way you send peaceful energetic threads to those connected to you.

CHAPTER 27

Service

I slept and dreamt that life was joy. I awoke and saw that life was service. I acted, and behold, service was joy.

— *RABINDRANATH TAGORE*

If you touch the lives of only a handful of others with a message of Oneness and Love, you will have made an incredible gift of your life here on earth, as life is service.

Let's start by sharing the spiritual spark we all have within us to create a brighter day. Take a minute to breathe in this moment like a new book. Say hello to a new blank page, ready for us to inscribe. Ah, the freshness of a new beginning in which we can create positive change in our world. Let us author peace, understanding, and happiness. Reach out a hand of help to those in need, because by helping others we help ourselves. Shine our Light and greet the new sunrise with blessings for a new day.

With awakening comes a deep call to selfless service. The call is slow at first, then it surges, a euphony within the heart, a message to you to help humanity with your gifts and strengths. On the path of spiritual maturity the call of selfless service strengthens your heart's receptive qualities as you let go of the barriers you build to protect your heart and feel the needs of others.

*I release myself to be of service with heart-centered authenticity
because I am excited about the promise life holds.*

I am enthusiastic about life and I look forward to change and growth. I give up anxiety and fear, yet I hold an intention for a brighter tomorrow, which fills me with overflowing gratitude and love. I understand that as we believe, we receive. Our connection to the Divine within allows us to manifest our physical reality. I understand that hope and love are great gifts I can bring to my selfless service of forgiveness and caring. The spirit of Oneness brings me harmony.

This world in which we live teaches by surrounding and infusing us with truths. We only need to open ourselves to know these truths.

Replenishment of our Being and unconditional giving are some of the truths the world gives us, and when we act in kind, we flow with the natural rhythm, the pulse of giving of oneself. As we give we benefit by seeing the beauty and freedom of giving and thus undergo a constant renewal of our Being. Find within that renewal of unselfish love: it is your essence.

Awaken your spiritual nature to life and dispel the self-centered grasping that is always at the expense of others. Share your essence of loving-kindness so mankind's positive nature may grow and benefit.

Our potential is so great. When we focus, allowing all distractions of past and future to fall away, eventually concepts of success and failure evaporate in the mists. Imbued with insight and clear attention we can accomplish more in service.

We should on occasion evaluate our spiritual practice to re-enlist and devote our service to humanity and the earth. From time to time we need to add new vigor to our disciplines to maintain a fresh vitality. This is a good time to see how the world sparkles with the beauty of nature, or human love. It is a good thought that this is the common theme to which we all contribute, bringing the Light of Love from our inner stillness to the world.

There is hope for what is considered a disturbed and broken human race. That hope lies within each of us, working in concert, awakening our compassionate higher being. We all must express love, because it is our responsibility to overcome and dissolve the distress and suffering. The world around you may seem like a raging sea, but by using loving compassion we learn to ride the waves and allow them to carry us toward our life of purpose.

Quan Yin in the Buddhist tradition is deity of mercy, and a bodhisattva. She is an example of compassion and service toward those suffering in this world of distraction.

We are always healing while on the path to spiritual maturity.

When we aid each other in the pursuit of healing, genuine accept-ance and caring are needed. Healing others requires healing oneself, and being sensitive to your own strengths, weaknesses, and truths.

Daily, we fortify our being with stillness and fill our being with Love and Light. There is much pain in the world and many times that pain reaches our heart, causing a disturbance. Before you act re-member that your nature is not pain, and that knowing your essence can make positive change. We all experience pain and suffering in life; it is a part of our physical existence. The way we reduce the pain and suffering in our own lives and others' is with our call to service. Showing compassion, joy, and gratitude are ways to serve and reduce pain and suffering.

When you push your personal agenda you can lose touch with your receptive self, which is connected to the Universal All. When you are receptive to the needs of those around you, and use imagina-tion, you can clearly see the best path. By being present and form-ing new ideas or images of service we present new potentials for the heart of humanity. Through stillness we move closer, with clarity and direction, to hear our personal message. Then, like ringing a bell, a universal message comes through the din of our mind, which tells us, "Learn to Love Everyone."

CHAPTER 28

Heart-Centered

*The mysteries of resonance and time vibrate in our essence.
Past, present, and future spiritual teachers work within higher
frequencies. When we are exposed to their frequencies, they
throb in our hearts, and once we achieve more acceleration in
our vibration, our hearts ring with Love like striking a bell.*

A crucial stage of human awareness is moving beyond intellectual
development into heart-centered consciousness. With higher
frequencies of consciousness we help every person that comes into
our lives. Look at the beauty and Light in each person you interact
with today, tomorrow, and every day. Once our heart-centered consciousness is awakened we truly step forward and start living.

Take comfort knowing there are many more that hear the call
of living spiritual, heart-centered lives. Every one of us, whether we
are aware or not, are learning ways to achieve and awaken our Being
in order to live authentically. We are not alone, and together we can
grow and support one another. We can help each other climb out of
this human box we have created; we need only to open our hearts to
find the path back into the Light.

Let us use heart-centeredness in our creativity, and empower the
present moment with positive intentions for tomorrow.

Listening with our heart opens the capacity for understanding and growth.

As we listen with our heart we develop greater creativity, generosity, empathy, and love. Listening this way creates stability within us for acceptance and tolerance. We become better equipped to flow with shifts and thus create better outcomes. But before we go deeper into our hearts we must make peace with the unresolved memories of the past that cause us anxiety. We cannot turn away from our hearts — this only creates more distance from the Divine. To discover what the unresolved memories of the past are we seek guidance from our heart. With understanding of past wounds we can bring peace into our mindful practice.

Every time we express some aspect of Divinity we align ourselves with Universal Oneness. Every action we perform leaves an imprint, or potential, on our subtle mind, and each potential eventually becomes its own karmic change. We can release the dark clouds of our past by moving positively with heart-centered intentions into this moment. The more effort we make toward living with heart-centered intentions the more we align our Being with Oneness. Spiritual maturity is never lost… Soul-Spirit unity is a mystical marriage.

Listen through your heart… Speak through your heart… Live through your heart…

When we allow our hearts to play our song, we strike a note with the Universe of Love. Resonating beyond our imagination with vastness, our heart's song shows its complexity and also its simplicity. Oneness weaves our song into the world's shift toward awakening. Allow your hearts to be filled to overflowing with the Light of Oneness. Allow your shimmering vessels to shine the glory of serenity, joy, peace, and love.

Find your joy and compassion then express it. Remove the many layers of protection from your heart — your heart is so amazingly powerful it needs no shielding. Allow the heart to experience life and be filled with beauty, thankfulness, and positivity; that is all the protection you need. Heart-centered people overcome the negativity of the world with love and compassion, in thoughts and deeds. Our hearts are so much stronger than we give credit, and when we open our hearts to the world they become even stronger.

Are we trying to live with Love in our hearts, loving one another, respecting our differences, and working toward peaceful communities based on assistance? We all have within us the ability to be of service in some way, so focus on living with Love.

Share your abundant spirit as part of the unending cycle of giving and receiving love.

Move through life with certainty and empowerment, knowing your actions are taking you toward purpose-filled events.

Sometimes it is best if we distance ourselves from undesirable life situations, so our Being can recover presence and renew with fresh strength. Establish new practices that are rooted in heart-centered intentions, which are present from this moment to the next. One step at a time, without expectation, allows life to take its own magnificent, elaborate shape and form. Remember the importance of self-control by taking time in the day to allow silence to calm you in heart-centered meditation. Working from a compassionate, loving, and disciplined heart is necessary for harmony. With loving intentions, see everything clearly, in bright and wondrous colors.

Live heart-centered, so you no longer live a self-centered life. Love consciousness creates humility, allowing us to nurture our sense of purpose and live a life of significant service. The more we appreciate simplicity the more heartfelt our understanding becomes. Our individual experiences unfurl Eternal Truth as fresh and new. Sway with the rhythm of life, pulsing your positive heartfelt intentions into the world. Feel the Mother of Life with the touch of your feet on the ground. Be one, interconnected with all life, honoring our Source.

CHAPTER 29

Loving Intentions

Help me to speak with clear and understandable intentions, and help me to listen to that which is significant, read what is meaningful, avoid the unnecessary, and make each word come from my heart.

The power of intention depends on your belief in yourself. Believe that you can simply "Be Love," "Be Joy," "Be." The more we return to our natural state of Being and Truth, the more energy our intention is given to become reality. Modify yourself toward positive loving intentions; after all we are connected to a unified universe of potentials. Who we are is changeless, birthless, and deathless. *Life is not what you see, but what is projected. It is not what is forged, but what is allowed.*

The building blocks of our world contain multiple dimensions of energy; they create what we perceive outside ourselves and within ourselves, with the assistance of intentions. Ask yourself: Am I considering the highest good in my intentions? Am I building my future with spiritual integrity? Keep your focus on heart-centered intentions because within each of us is a spark of perfection that exists for eternity. This spark has a silent pulse that connects us to the multiple dimensions of reality. When we gaze into our Light we no longer see our shortcomings; instead we see the unity and rhythm of the universe. Use this connection to transform your worldview into harmonious loving intentions.

Love is the great purifier on the higher planes of existence.

Strengthen the connection of your Divine Light, and hold up your intentions in its purifying illumination. Allow your intentions to be tested and refined and you will find the best path to proceed for the good of all. When we truly know what it is in this life we are supposed to do or be, we need only to affirm with loving intention, and see ourselves in that place. When our affirmations are in alignment with our purpose, the universe will assist by arranging our path so we can accomplish our goals.

Life is providing for us, yet are we available to hear, see, feel, or sense the gifts that surround us? Follow the flow. Unfurl your magnificence, allowing the flow of the Universe to stream through your being. The nature of life is to grow. Become all that is possible by cultivating loving intentions so you can simply *Be*.

To build a positive lifestyle with positive experiences, review all aspects of this life with pure intentions. Even when something does not go our way, view it with deliberate positivity. We have been given the power of desiring or declining and pursuing or avoiding, and each and every one of us knows within the correct choices. We are only tempered clay and water but our decisions send an energetic action forward that will resonate for eons. Take time to bless the ones you love with your open heart. Deeply express yourself with loving intentions, sending unconditional love.

Set your intentions with loving care aligned with service and you will fulfill your purpose.

Every action does have a reaction, so the intention you set today will manifest in its time. Let each part of your life have its time. Slowly, ever so slowly, we forge a life of loving intentions by increasing our positive thoughts and emotions. Allow your Being's Light to shine through shadows, solidifying the presence of Love.

It is time we create heartlands, communities of heart-centered individuals dedicated to the purpose of reducing suffering and promoting unity. It is time for action, to let go of apathy within our communities and get involved. Express yourself from your center of loving intentions and respect for others. Develop loving intentions for positive empowering change in our communities; work toward cooperation, improving health, and strengthening stability.

Let us use our intentions to create synergy in our world with our love, compassion, and awakened consciousness. The Light shines on all of us when we work together with heart-centered loving intentions. The barriers we built in the past will come down when we act with pure intention of service. The Universe will aid us in achieving what is the greater good for mankind.

We have infinite possibilities that are inherent in our divine creative self to build quality communities that support all.

Within our hearts strides a young golden lion or lioness, with unlimited potential. Every movement is grace, your vision is creative, your smile radiates love, and your compassion is healing. Walk in the sunny breeze of abundance sharing your heart's essence and connection to Spirit.

Remember: our objective in life is to become the best we can be, with loving intention and compassion for others. Carry this vibration, this energy, through your day, and do it with simplicity, peace, and joy. We are, after all, interconnected Beings that make up a collective whole, so when we choose a life of loving intention we strengthen the human potential of Love. Help others step out of the darkness by bringing loving intention to all you do to create positive change.

An awakened heart will expand and create space for the future by living with loving intention in this moment. An awakened heart will expand its capacity to love and not be limited by ego identity, allowing Light to reach all parts of your Being. There is no boundary between you and those around you; you do not need to take in the drama others may generate.

Keep true to your essence of loving intention; do not let someone else's ego pull you away from mindfulness. Feel the flow of those around you, touch them gently with your love, and assist them in positive, empowering goals. Assistance can help others break free from the confines of ego and live more in harmony with Universal Oneness.

CHAPTER 30

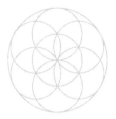

Love

There is a great need for Love in the world, and we are the seeds to make it grow. For Love to happen in the world, it must first arise from the deepest core of our Being. Let Love's vibration become you.

Live in Love and all your labor will be Love, eliminating sorrow and desire. Our highest value derives from what we give, in what we do for others, and in how we care for this planet. The Buddha said, *"Live in Love. Do your work. Make an end of your sorrows."* Are we connecting to our Divine Nature so that we may live in Love and understand what our work really is? Connect to your Source and know the joyous work of Love this life holds for you, work that will fill your heart with purpose.

Living in Love keeps the heart open. No one can harm an open heart filled with Love. In this way we release suffering. Some are anxious about going within and reaching toward the Oneness. Yet is it not natural for us to find vibrations that strengthen our Being? When we find our Love and compassion we unite with our True Being, and become part of the Oneness.

Beloved, Be-Loved, Be Loved. Every time we see beauty, kindness, and recognize goodness in simple things, we experience being loved.

Love is the unifying language of the universe. It is the glue that binds our vibratory atoms into this form we know as you and me. If there is only one thing our ego minds have to grasp on to in life, let it be Love. We come from the Light like a young person new from school into active life. Yet how soon we forget all we knew. Like a student, we wander through life looking for Love until we remember — Love is not thought. Love is experienced and felt always in our Being. Once remembered, we are again reborn and then we can present our whole self to this life.

Allow more Love simply by experiencing it. Appreciate the loving-kindness you feel toward others; allow it to radiate outward. Be loved and allow your heart to be filled with Love for everyone and everything. It is Love that radiates from you into all that is. Feel this aliveness, this expanded space both inward and outward. Feel it when listening to another; feel it when looking at the stars, trees, and flowers. Inhabit your body with this expansive feeling and allow it to be your connection to wholeness.

Always keep Love at hand. Keep love with you always, in decision making, in work, and play. Find the Love in your core essence, and shine it so all can see you live in Love.

We are the brush that colors our world, and Love illuminates
our creations. We remember though, that we are neither
the master nor owner of what we create. We are here only to
participate in the creation.

There are messages all around us, in the whispers of the leaves, the call of a dove, an unexpected rainbow. Love is everywhere. Keeping focused and steady with Love in our hearts, sustains us in the universal flow, as we contribute loving intentions to others. Love is all around us, yet many of us have to learn how to receive Love. Spiritual experiences show us a way, the doorway to the unbound Divine Love that is in everything. All we have to do is learn how to open our hearts and *Be* our authentic selves.

At the core of our Universe is Love. Each of us has felt it and longed for it in our hearts. Yet our minds do not understand Love, this invisible force that calls to us. Love tells us to accept ourselves, love ourselves, and give love naturally in everything we do. Love is awakened consciousness. Love is the core of our Being and we sometimes get carried away with our thinking to such a point that we lose track of it.

When we are attuned to the natural flow of love in our Being, we awaken our sense of insight, which will guide us through our tasks and toward our purpose. Allow Love to be the only power at work in your heart and life because the greatest gift we can give is being able to give Love freely with no thought of what we may receive in return. When we give freely from our Divine center, we see the Divine in all, and ultimately receive by giving. Every interaction we have in this life is an opportunity to give Love and receive Love. Every loving action leads us toward achieving and fulfilling our heartfelt purpose.

Smiles bring warmth to our hearts on a cold night.
Laughter brings joy to a community struggling to get by.
Love brings connection to a world separated by fear and the
unknown. Smile warmly and give freely of laughter until your
heart opens with unconditional love.

There is one unifying ideal we all share and that is unconditional
Love. Some of us have had an exceptional loving experience, while
many are wondering when or how to find it. We do not have to wait
for that magic to happen; we can learn to cultivate Love in our lives
now.

To the level that we practice Love, we should feel the presence
of Oneness within. All life is consciousness and awareness of our
participation with Divine Love. Let us build our Love, Truth, Self-
Acceptance, Tolerance, and Gratitude knowing these aspects are part
of the I Am Consciousness. Our Light is alive with Love Consciousness. Sharing and shining our Love with all Beings allows us to feel
the touch of Love reaching outward toward everything in the Universe. We feel it reaching toward parent and child, sister and brother,
friend to friend, and from our Being to our Mother Earth. Dissolve
your cares in the love for this moment and be totally present.

Recognition of Love brings a deep contentment and knowing that
something precious has been stored deep within our hearts.

CHAPTER 31

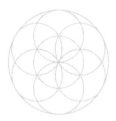

Light

We are like the person who searches all night by candlelight for a little fire. We are like the person on mule-back who searches the land to find a mule. Searching, searching, searching, when the Light is within.

In this present moment we have access to the power of life itself. Within each of us is our connection, a connection to our higher consciousness that resides within the Light. Embracing this makes it a living reality in our lives, so we may witness Light Consciousness manifesting in every moment of our lives. Once the Light has been awakened and brought into our reality, we cannot go back. The true gift is sharing your Light. Let us keep the Light burning within.

May we all keep peace and happiness in our hearts, may we all keep peace and happiness for our families, may we all keep peace and happiness for our communities, and may we all keep peace and happiness for the world. Let the transformation begin within our hearts and flow through us to spread outward. May our hearts become like pearled drops of Light to illuminate the darkness.

In this storm of humanity, be the shining beacon of Light that helps reduce suffering. Firmly grounded in this reality, shine a clear vision of strength, hope, and awakening to keep others from turbulent waters.

We absorb Light into our Being all the time, constantly refreshing and renewing. Our Being also emits our Light, which is then absorbed by all things and all other beings. We are constantly exchanging and changing Light with the Universe, giving us new potentials. In this way our consciousness works with the Universe to determine our future.

As we let our Light shine, without realizing it, we give others permission to do the same. Have you noticed when your joy inside is bursting to the surface it affects all who are around you? This is because when we release our fear to just *BE*, it allows others to release their fear and be themselves. Our Light shines through and connects the way in which it is intended. When we are connected to our Light this way, we step out into the world shining it ever so brightly. It is the interconnection others feel and reflect, illuminating the source for empowering change.

Recall various life decisions that held the same higher principles you know from the Light. Become the lantern burning brightly, a radiant beacon, by living the ideals and dedicating Truth. Communicate with everything in the world through your Light. The rocks, plants, sun, and stars all reveal their interconnected nature in your Light. Brighten the gloom of this moment and the next with your Light.

Now is the time to activate Love and Light in your life. Creating, loving, and sharing actualize the qualities of the Divine in everyday activities. Deliver your Pure Light for a shining future.

Come shimmering Light into my heart. Fill me with pure, unselfish, and loving Light. Allow my actions and words to spill out the loving Light of Oneness into all my interactions.

There is Light within each of us that flows even through the darkest places, ever-present and available to us for support, knowing, and Love. Our mind sees this as a myth, yet our heart dissolves those thoughts of myth with Truth. Light emerges within us like the sun peaking above a mountain at sunrise. Brighter and brighter light slowly illuminates the shadows so we can see the clearly defined borders. Light helps us see who we are, and strengthen who we will become.

Allow your Light to lead you in the flow of Oneness. Your Light is a pure high-energy state that provides enthusiasm in your heart and brilliance and clarity in your mind. Discover the reality of your Light, which is stronger than you ever imagined. Our Being is luminescent and gives off Light that touches the stars and mingles and merges with the Universe. Our Light increases our self-confidence and strengthens our minds with our life's potentials, formulating into new ideas for our future.

May the essence of the Light seep into your being so you achieve a loving nature with peace at your core. The Love and compassion of the Light are timeless and boundless, transcending our physical limits, lifting us up from our mire.

Let your Light build within until the seeds of knowledge are ripe and complete to be let loose upon the winds. Allow the seeds of light to float wherever they are needed for the greatest good in the world.

Enlightenment means to become full of Light, open to the Divine Oneness, allowing the Light to touch our hearts. We can read, study, and acquire intellectual knowledge, yet is that truly knowing? In stillness we find what has been forgotten and what we are now ready to receive. Is that knowing? In the Light we have access to all that is, and all that will be — it is part of our Being, our Knowing.

There is nothing comparable in this physical existence to the Light. We manage to glimpse the Infinite Divine and we cannot even begin to describe it. We realize the Light is our continual source of Love, Joy, Intelligence, and Truth, all gifts to be experienced, and yet the Light is beyond our vocabulary.

To describe Light is to limit it to our linear perspective. We all know where to find it, because it dwells within us, within the stillness, within All. Once a glimpse of Light is planted it must be left to open and expand naturally.

All spiritual practices are good, especially when performed through heart-centered loving intention. Care should be taken though, if we fuss with our seed of light with our ego minds we disrupt its growth.

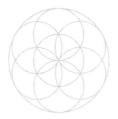

CHAPTER 32

Mindfulness

May I stay mindful during the seemingly routine, day-to-day life, because Truth and Beauty are often right there in front of me, awaiting a wondrous moment of discovery.

This is our life story, precious and dear, so how focused are we during most of it? Often we repeat actions without much thought and sometimes we unintentionally hurt others or ourselves. Let us transform anger into gentleness and use that energy for positive growth. We unconsciously throw around huge amounts of energy. Let us focus on the energy we are exchanging with the Universe using mindfulness. When we develop a mindful, focused lifestyle we will give all of ourselves in everything we do.

Mindfulness can be focused upon anytime, during any activity. Wherever you live or work mindfulness is key to the whole development of heart and mind. In all you do, practice being in this moment in your body, your feelings, your mind, and the products of your mind. Be present and find the concentration and loving wisdom of wholeness. Mindfulness keeps us focused on what is in front of us so that we may fully experience the present moment. Mindfulness helps us to surrender the notion of individuality to become aware of the consciousness that flows through all things.

Observe reality in the world and in yourself. Be aware of what is going on in your body, your feelings, and your mind.

Mindfulness helps us develop concentration and insight to see reality as it is. This helps the turbulent waves of our physical existence to wash over us, not affecting us as much. Keep your connection to the universal flow of Unity, Light, and Love and its constantly changing, new, and wonderful experiences.

Our life is a journey down a long, infinite path that extends into the future. Through mindfulness experience the textures of your path and everything surrounding you in the present moment.

Knowing our interconnection we realize that our hearts contain the whole world. The higher reality of our True Being may be difficult for our dull senses to fully grasp, but it reveals itself in the smallest details of our daily lives. You will see and learn more through a daily mindful discipline of being present, staying alert even while doing tedious and routine daily tasks.

At the same time look beyond the task to your environment, and surrounding areas and take in all the details. With practice you will soon find that what you do in heightened awareness becomes interesting and enjoyable as you begin to see a greater picture. Notice the connection between everything in any given moment. By looking beyond yourself you see the inner dimension of consciousness flowing into every situation.

Mindfully breathe, passing through and around obstacles, like the wind on a prairie passes through a fence. Mindfully breathe a song of love and compassion into the winds for the greater good.

The Universe may be one with me, but am I one with the Universe? This is an early question of a student. We all have distractions that knock us off center and pull us away from the present. What matters is how quickly we can return to our center. Are we moving from non-being to Being?

Enjoy the bliss of Being today and every day as you walk without worry, anxiety, depression, or despair. Appreciate your place in this world. Find contentment and aliveness in where you are going and what you are doing. Peace comes when there is inner harmony, so listen to the rhythm of your own metronome, your heartbeat.

Harmonize with the outer world by feeling your pulse. Soften your physical and emotional condition with harmony. When looking at our world see the beauty of nature all around you, as well as people and situations. See the qualities, potential, and larger issues in all your interactions in order to make harmonious and wise decisions. Allow your glance to be creative and filled with Light, and then watch as change unfolds.

Strengthen your bridge to Spirit by being present. Nurture a simple mindfulness practice.

Mindfulness lets you see and notice more detail in every experience. When we focus on our five senses of sight, smell, hearing, taste, and touch, it keeps us in this moment. Introduce a sixth sense, of listening to your intuitive mind. Let Spirit guide you. By focusing your awareness you quiet the mind and experience an expansion of consciousness. By being present you reinforce the bridge that was always there but may have been weakened from inattention. Add a structural support of mindful presence to your day and reopen the bridge of connection to Oneness.

Take time to see through the mists we call reality. Take time to find the calm still center of your Being where clarity is discovered. With mindful attention see your Truth with clarity. If we come to live and understand our spiritual nature, then our physical reality flows much easier. Everything we learn through mindfulness about the world and ourselves, we bring back to our heart and practice. Breathe in the recognition of your True Self and become friends.

As we walk our path in life, it appears as a spiral, always moving upward, and we cannot see around the next turn. Even though the path gets steeper and is ever turning away, if we practice mindfulness, we will be able to appreciate the decreased radius and our increased focus helps us know our path.

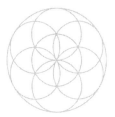

CHAPTER 33

Gratitude

Opening my eyes, I am grateful for a new dawn and a day full of wonder. I am but a drop in the ocean of humanity connected to all. It is unnecessary to feel more because we are One.

The gratitude of, "Thank you for this life" is a good way to start each day. Living in gratitude helps to see the need in others, and allows us to be of service. Gratitude and service hold each hand of Love. Think about giving thanks for our Mother Earth; during this life we walk on her with admiration and respect. This teaches us to respect all life.

As we walk through life let us maintain gratitude and a thankful spirit. Recall that we all share a common purpose — to help humanity return to loving unity and respect for our Mother Earth. Radiate this calm purpose from your heart and pass it on to others.

Let us honor our connection with Spirit with gratitude and Love. Our connection is a self-perpetuating sphere of consciousness. When we act together with Spirit we awaken unlimited divine expansion toward harmony and Oneness. An awakened state of life is an experience of being present with clarity and gratitude, which expresses itself as a flow of love. We feel this is how life should be lived, free of negative ego and emotional drama…. I am grateful for the opportunity to make empowering choices that point me toward being present. I am grateful for my connection to unity and Oneness.

*Bring the sacred into our everyday tasks. Look toward the
horizon and see the magnificence of life.*

There is only one ceremony and it is life. All of the other rituals we
do along the way are meant to remind us of the greater ceremony. If
we start each day with gratitude and stillness, then our walk through
the day becomes one of connection to all people, places, and things.
We see what is really important and focus on our core roles. Our
every thought and action affects the fabric of creation and thus our
every tomorrow. Treat each moment with sacred respect and vitalize
the great ceremony of life.

Start or end the day with the resolve to strengthen your Being.
The first few moments of awakening are boundless with potential
for programming the day with empowerment. Take advantage of a
rested mind, and fill it with thoughts of gratitude, love, and compassion. As you continue to prepare for your day, center by rejoicing in
being a part of this great universe. Within each of us are works of
divine providence, so we should give praise to the Divine Source in
all that we do.

The last few moments of a day hold the opportunities of review-
ing the day with sacred respect and reverence. Sing a hymn of gratitude as you do your work and other daily chores.

One who lives in desire has trouble being grateful. Meaning is the greatest hunger for mankind. Look toward your True Nature for meaning, so you may live in gratitude.

Let us not imagine something lacking when our needs create an imaginary hole of wants in our heart. Move forward fulfilled, knowing the entire universe moves forward with you. Find meaning and gratitude in this moment, this day, this life.

My thoughts often turn to gratitude for the abundance I've been given. It is so important to take the time to appreciate the small and large things in life and give thanks to those who fill our days with love and compassion. Thank you to my community of peace-loving friends and collaborators for being a part of my life on the path to wholeness in our lives. You are doing a wonderful job.

Living simply with less distraction is the direction of gratitude and focus.

Look at what is really important in life. We are all a piece of the Oneness. We are not an accumulation of stuff we own or a persona we developed to be more popular. We are going to get what we need, not what we think we need. Eventually we begin to know we only need what we have in this moment. If we live in gratitude then we are satisfied, and we will succeed in every moment of our path toward purpose.

As we progress on our spiritual path we are grateful for the stages of progress in others and ourselves. We recognize and appreciate the mark of authentic spiritual experiences in others and value deep friendship among kindred souls who aspire to the same destination.

CHAPTER 34

Compassion

*Be open to the world around, breathe and feel the heartbeat,
the natural rhythm that pervades everything. Feel compassion.*

Allow life to be what it is and be a participant, be a co-creator. We have so much life to live and we are able to convey it in a flow of compassion. Extend your heart of hearts toward your fellow citizen. The loving force within moves all things toward harmony and wholeness. Look inward for pure love, where it is strong, so when you act with pure love it becomes compassion.

It may appear as if we are all from different cultures but we are all the same inside. Open up to feel someone else's journey with pure love and compassion and you open a path of light. Compassion is seeing and feeling someone else as one with you, it is what brings us together. Listen and feel from a place of compassion and a whole new sphere of connection awaits.

Enjoy a life filled with Compassion.

Are we trying to become actors rather than real people? It is like storing your essence in a jar where only a select few may glimpse it. Live within your truth, virtue, and honesty. The key to authenticity is living with heart-centered compassion and intention.

Know that you are becoming more loving and compassionate. React by living life to its fullest and believe life has a purpose, even if that purpose is at times obscure. Invariably, purpose involves love of family and community or service to others. Know that the love you create will be reflected back in everyone and everything. Immerse yourself in the flow of life; accept the swirling world around you. In that place of peace you can change the world toward love and compassion.

From the Light of absolute perfection we receive blessings of inner peace that softens our hearts so we may build compassion. We share our blessings with a world hungry for peaceful solutions.

Every life situation teaches us something and we have an obligation to the world that brought us up, to grow from it. We can't cover our face or turn away from suffering, because the situations will continue to be there. We have to relate to the world and deal with the distractions with an enlightened heart and mind, with wisdom and compassion.

When we speak about living life with loving intention and purity of heart, it seems so simple. In difficult times it's not easy to maintain compassionate actions: if before we react impulsively we connect with our inner peace we can then respond with compassion.

Our hearts swell with joy and love as we give thanks for all blessings and gifts that present themselves in our lives. It may seem counter-intuitive but we owe gratitude even to those people who provide irritation, negativity, and demands. They have provided us with real world training to build our compassion and keep us grounded in this world. They inspire us to find peaceful, and spiritual solutions to the hard questions.

I am grateful that deep within is a flower that purifies pride, desire, and aggression. The flower within grants wisdom, compassion, love, and a wish to become enlightened.

From hearts of Love comes a spiral of compassion that fuels the Universe. The act of compassion is never ending; it is a bloom that once opened continues to expand. Change your perception to realize everything you experience is a gift. Notice the warmth, love and compassion within your heart, feel the sense of connection to the world around.

Activate the full force of this steady, calm, and infinite grace that is your loving heart. This is the divine power that flows through and beyond you, giving compassion and commitment. A balanced heart gives love and compassion like a cup filled to the rim and overflowing, always feeling love and always giving love. When we open our heart, our love merges with all the love in the universe and there we find compassion for everyone. Love is the one force that can grace us with compassion.

Create moments of stillness in the day, like spinning bubbles of love and compassion. Give way to cooperation and unity consciousness, then we can support each other. In these moments of stillness see how the thoughts of "I" are removed and merge into "We."

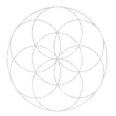

CHAPTER 35

Interconnection

I AM all of me. I AM this physical presence, I AM my True Nature, I AM interconnected to All. I consist of my actions, words, thinking, and reality — all contributing to the totality of that which is I AM.

The *Tao Te Ching* tells us that all being originates in non-being. We are inherently all original beings from one Source. In stillness we find our interconnection to the Oneness and thus to all other original beings. We are what we come from and we come from Oneness. We are all interconnected on so many levels: energetic, subatomic, and within the Light. The process of working together toward the same ends strengthens our interconnection, moving everyone forward and thus strengthening our connection to Oneness.

Let us change our perspective from being an individual just surviving, toward being interconnected and of service to all. Notice the differences between people and accept those differences. The differences are what make us capable of doing great things together. Ask yourself: What do I need to change so differences no longer matter? Life is all about feeling the greater connection to all and being of service. It is no longer about me, instead it is all about *us*. Find your connection in whatever way is comfortable and feel the vibration that will steer you toward awakening.

We live in a spiritual universe, where unity and Spirit are present in everything. Our interconnection is a great truth, needing more exploration.

Science has been searching for the keys to life, yet we only have to go within to find the consciousness that is our spark, our Light. What we have been searching for is in all of us and in all things. Our Light may only be a fragment of Oneness, yet it is interconnected and looking upon itself. Recognize your connection to everything in the Universe, and understand that when you flow with your connection you are ONE. Move harmoniously with the Universe, with heaven and Earth, and allow it to show the way.

Being interconnected to everything, we can use a simple stone or plant, to bring us back to Oneness and becoming whole. Without imposing any of your thoughts, open your awareness to a plant or stone and allow its essence to communicate and reveal itself. Then, as you commune more deeply, notice within that essence a reflection of you. We are all part of an infinite Universe, and we must not allow the magnitude of it to make us feel insignificant.

We may not see the big picture, yet we need to believe we have a purpose. Understanding we have a place in the world helps us to ignite Love, so we may live with joy and harmony.

Which is more conscious, the butterfly, or the flower? We are all doing the best we can with what we have been given. Whether we stretch our wings or are rooted and firm with the earth and elements, we are all interconnected and interdependent on each other to make this world a better place.

We sometimes feel held in bondage to our physical bodies, chained to this physical world of distraction and separateness; we feel confined and led by our egos. So the biggest challenge in today's world is overcoming self-centered egotism. We are only here for a short time and do not need to empower self-centered thinking. Unshackle our separateness with a daily practice of contemplation, connecting to the Divine within and find your unfettered True Nature. Then begin living for all beings.

Savor the loss of animosity; attain the empty feeling of letting go. Whenever we completely let go we soar beyond a grasping ego, no longer seeing ourselves as I, but as our transcendent Light. Fill our ego with Love and interconnection with everyone and every thing. This sweet resonance dissolves our wants and needs into contentment of being.

Open your heart essence to new innovation. Share your energy with everyone.

Our higher connection is not on an external level, because externally we perceive shapes and forms; we see differences. With our inner perception we see the depths of our energy flowing as One with our Universe. We are multifaceted beings with connection to all the elements. We are not attached to only one condition; we express different elements throughout the day and in our lives. We know our world better and more effectively with a variety of experiences, broadening our knowing of the Divine in stillness and in life.

As we become one with life, we find within each of us all the elements of our Universe. Ground yourself in your True Nature, release the stress, and be content with life.

The greatest changes for humanity are made up of threads of relationships that are woven together into a fabric of interconnectivity which bring about new insights. There is a thread in each of us that all life flows through. To find that fiber in yourself try feeling connected to every person you encounter. Connect to nature and practice Love and non-judgment.

Remember, we are a part of the Oneness and we are Love. We are all interconnected, so keeping a positive and loving intention through life is key to changing our world. Do not forget to love the upset and hurt parts of yourself first.

CHAPTER 36

Community

We cannot live our lives in a bubble. To effect real change strive to see the world and our community with clear vision.

We live in a paradigm of heroic individuals struggling over limited resources, yet do we always need the biggest, the fastest, the best? What we do need is a new story, so that we can live in harmony and within our means, establishing cooperation, and building on our dynamic relationships. Each of us affects everyone else. We can no longer live with the mentality of, "I win and you lose." Instead adopt the fresh philosophy of, "I win and we all win." We can correct injustices, and the best place to start is by developing clear vision to see the world we live in.

We work toward helping each other so we can transcend the enormous shifts we face in the world. Yet should the members of any society become so homogeneous that all traces of cultural diversity vanish? No, No, No!! Honor cultural diversity to build a future of unity and community. Adapt, and let us move forward together.

One of the most important contributions we can make to the political, social, and economic issues of today is to recognize that we all need each other to bring about a state of Universal Peace. We are all interdependent and share a bond of divine unity with each other.

Develop openness in body, speech, and mind. See yourself as this world. With a larger vision there is no need for boundaries and nothing to fight over. With a larger vision there is respect for all parts of the whole.

Diversity builds strength. Take a look at a circle: it faces 360 degrees looking outward and inward in all directions. Our family, our community, our world, and ourselves can all be viewed as circles within circles. The circle symbolizes many things — the Absolute, enlightenment, strength, elegance, the Universe, and the Void. Let us develop a circle of diversity, respecting and accepting, always knowing that in the center of our circle is Peace, Love, and Light.

You have spent time to connect with your heart center and develop gratitude for this moment, now move even further, to create greater cooperation and generosity in your community. Using your 360-degree heart center circle transform from me into *WE*.

WE develop compassion in our daily practice. *WE* care that someone in our town is suffering. *WE* care that millions are suffering all over the world. *WE* care that our Earth is changing and apathy is only making it worse.

Bring your voice to your community and plant the seeds of transformation.

Emulate the ideas of an enlightened society. Work together to uplift your existence and that of others without disrespecting others' beliefs or faith. It is a gift for us to act on our shared awakening consciousness. Many of us are beginning to see the value of community. The energy we share is helping us to build a greater empathic center in our world.

We have a shared responsibility of working together. Moving forward is all about taking risks. The ultimate risk is sharing your authentic self as you work toward a brighter time to come. You start within, and then share with your circle so you may all work together in harmony. See your Self in the place of another. Engage, and develop within your society support for others, co-creating dynamic strong communities of cooperation friendship and mutual respect.

Help to find or create community with like-minded individuals and generate positive empowering outcomes of enlightenment. Give the gift of loving intention, friendship, and camaraderie. Link to other communities in peaceful co-existence for the benefit of humanity. Caring people living a life of service make a difference.

As each of us gathers strength from heart-centered unity we become champions for change in our communities. It is time for advocacy of change.

Each of us can instill heart-centered loving intentions into our work and businesses. Using heart-centered business models helps humanity and our world sustain a healthy, whole environment. Return compassion and caring to the workplace; be a forward-thinking leader. It takes great inner strength, courage, and self-confidence to go against social pressures to act with loving intention in all we do. Our society is only beginning to understand the importance of living a heart-centered life.

Do not fear helping someone birth a new idea of loving intention. Collaborate by bringing your time, energy, and support to any heart-centered project. As we bring more of these ideas to fruition we are creating a better world. May we stay centered in our being and in our doing, so we may come together as a heart-centered community, building responsibility to each other, and helping to sustain each other's awakenings. As we work on our personal growth, it will contribute to the collective energies of us all.

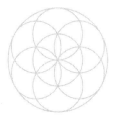

CHAPTER 37

A Shift

Living as authentic Beings we observe tides and shifts that give us opportunities for new perspectives. A huge wave of change is upon us; we have felt the shudders of its approach. Prepare to be flexible, allowing the drama to flow past, a discipline that helps our future.

Many of us from time to time reach a point of feeling as if we are in some sort of standby stage. Although we strive to follow a path of consciousness and discovery, reading, learning and experiencing all that crosses our path, at times the path forward is not clear. Spirit's guidance tells us to wait and practice being patient, or just be at peace. Yet we know in our core that we should keep moving forward. We feel out of balance, so we return to our root teachings and attempt to center and clear the mind.

These periods in life are precursors of major energetic shifts that are looming; the Universe is spending this necessary time to align what is needed to facilitate that shift. In such a period it is best to work on integrating past experiences and life patterns, developing coherence with the heart, mind, and higher consciousness.

In this way you increase your resonance with the Universe as the shift happens and move forward with deep listening, harmony, reverence for life, and true happiness. This stage of standby really matters, especially if we use it for preparing ourselves.

A tremendous surge in energy has been building quietly under the surface; it cannot be contained, and a spark of Light will release it.

Often we feel we do not have a choice, that we must keep the status quo. Yet we are living in evolutionary times, and there is constant restlessness. Heart-centered engagement demands that we act and live with presence of the need for change. A shift comes when things can no longer change incrementally but must change fundamentally. When things no longer work we must rebuild from the basic elements.

We are creating a new world from the world of pure potential. Experience the flow of Spirit into the physical world. This process is happening continuously and we intensify it when it is part of our consciousness. Be aware of the essence of your being to develop Love, understanding, and compassion. See clearly and take a stand against oppression and injustice, creating positive, heart-centered change.

Change never comes to an end; it only varies in intensity. We need strong spiritual roots so when the winds of change blow we are able to bend in the gale. If we expand our consciousness, then we can spread our understanding and be a shining spark of Light that displays change can be for the better.

Breathe in the new dawn and let it fill you with Love, Hope, and Courage as we emerge from the darkness.

With the dawn we begin on a new road of Light and awakening. We all have a part to play in bringing a greater spiritual consciousness to our world. The loving intentions were laid down before our births and our children's children will know the completion.

Abundant energy is present to carry us into awakening. Look inside and see what is budding. In these shifting times we provide loving support for the dying paradigm while fostering and stimulating the emergence of conscious awakening. We have all that is needed to continue moving forward.

Change is always on the horizon, and the best we can do is to develop the ability and desire to change within ourselves. Embrace flexibility and reduce the fear of impermanence. Acknowledge the power and potential of change in our lives. Work to move beyond our old methods, because it is too easy to fall into old patterns. Step outside the circle of comfort and expand your boundaries by growing your empathic field. Choose to go the distance for others, helping us to become all we are capable of in communities of cooperation.

Little things add up, contributing to the shift in consciousness.
One drop can create hundreds of ripples.

Life is going so fast and change is coming so quickly that when Spirit guides us to act we do so without delay. We are where we are supposed to be, here to provide positive assistance and service. Start building your resilient future in this present moment by weaving new adaptive heart-centered energy into all that you do. Prepare for shifts by allowing your life to flow with the shift as it redesigns this moment. Your mental attitude is the most influential factor in working toward your goals. When you choose to create the shift within, you effect change in the world. Developing inner harmony is key to making a more peace-filled world.

There are no "separate" individuals, and as we pass through this long night into a new dawn we continue together as one. With deep longing to be reunited with the Light and Oneness, we step forward toward Unity and Awakening.

CHAPTER 38

Unity

Each is loved unconditionally beyond measure. Within Divine
Love is right action flowing naturally, in all ways, always.

A wave on the ocean can travel hundreds of miles but eventually it blends with the smooth surface of the sea and is gone. But the wave is not gone and more waves follow. Like the sea, we move with the flow of ebbs and tides. Our future is not fixed, rather it presents an array of possibilities. Let us move with Love and be a wave of eternal presence, always connected to the unifying energy.

The more we move away from our connection with nature, the more we disconnect with our True Being. It is too easy to get caught up in the techno world of man, thinking that is all there is to reality. Reflect on your connection to unity and your physical reality. Untie the knots of physical life through awakening consciousness. Your Being knows the way. Join a new order of humanity leading us out of the decline and gridlock we have created through our unskilled behaviors. Let us move toward positive and empowering integration.

We have the support of the Universe whether we acknowledge it or not. Within our hearts are echoes of Love's song.

There is a kinship among all who seek unity of the heart. When we live in Love, we become part of a love song, helping others find Love's echoes in their hearts. We honor and are grateful for Love, harmony, and beauty. Study the lessons of Nature and balance them between your heart and mind. Recognize the teacher everywhere, as we are always students.

A Divine principle within us joins with the Divine Universe. Look at the spark within and know the flame. Look for the Divine within so you will recognize the Divine in rocks, water, Earth, or her inhabitants. Take in more and more of the complexities of reality, until your bewilderment changes to simplicity. Allow the richness of reality to become one within your Being. Move with Nature until every cell of your body knows unity.

Color your life with hope, Love, and Light that unifies our world and Eternal Being. The way to an illuminated life is living life to the fullest, with support and joy for all.

The experience of unity is felt through all our senses. In quiet reflection we link to our Source, seeing the similarity between us in Spirit. Devotion to our spiritual being breaks the illusion of separateness. With contemplation we find a unity that gently holds the field of all possibilities. Within unity we connect to our inspiration and innovation, creating solutions needed to awaken humanity.

Breathe deeply of the unifying force behind the existence of all that is unity. Our spiritual destiny lies in recognizing that One and All are equal. Let us realize we do not have to accept evil in our communities. Breathe slowly for increasing spiritual connection in our world. The heaviness of life is lifted through the expansiveness of unity. Merge with the Universe to express and participate in the beauty of your Divine Essence so that you bring it into all you do, thus creating change.

The treasure of our daily practice is the journey of self-discovery. Down the same tracks as the ancient masters, we keep the knowledge of Love and compassion in our hearts, always moving ahead toward new realms of spirituality.

Our world calls us to connect with the loving intentions of our early spiritual founders, sages, and masters. They shared a desire for all Beings to find freedom, unity, and harmony, a knowing that teaches if we come together we can accomplish anything. Understand the deeper knowledge found in our spiritual nature, and share our Divinity.

On the higher levels of consciousness there is no difference between outer and inner. Spirit and matter are not separate; our physical form replicates the Universe, and its energy came together giving us embodiment. What is outside is within … Unity.

We all have a choice about how to continue on our paths. Fast or slow, alone or with others, we decide how to affect our future. Unblazed trails lie before you. Take with you only what is needed to sustain and always return what you can to maintain balance. Each of us has our own path and each of us will travel it in a particular way. Choose well as you blaze a new path for the unity of humanity.

CHAPTER 39

Observing with
Non-Attachment

How are we empowered? Not by others, but by becoming fully assured that we each are One with the Universal All. We face life's obstacles as participants and observers with loving intentions.

Why does clarity arise out of watchfulness? The more you watch, the more you are quieted within and slow down. Your chattering mind chatters less and, transmuted, allows an even keener watchfulness. This enhances the quality of the energy that always emanates from your essence.

Not being attached to your expectations of others frees you of frustration and disappointment. Not all will live up to your desired results, because they are simply living their own path, different from yours. Without living their path how can we presume to know another's outcome or direction?

As we move along life's path we often search for our rhythm. Patience and observation of what is occurring in life at this moment is key to our tempo. We attempt to be adaptive in our everyday circumstances because we cannot always count on singing the same song every day of our life. When we feel the rhythm of the moment we find ourselves easily flowing with the melodic beat. Then we contribute our own unique variations to the concert.

The Witness awakens, as your True Nature becomes known.
The Witness takes nothing and gives nothing, thus allowing
consciousness to expand its knowing.

Be an observer of life without naming things; it helps you to see more clearly. To name a thing attaches a preconceived notion to it. Every time we attach a notion to something we are attaching our energy, our vibration, and thus that which we observe is changed by our act of observation. Our act of observation, after all, is an action that creates a reaction. Our energy influences our unlimited potentials. Align your energy with the Universe and its multiple dimensions. By developing heart-centered action and mindfulness we expand our potentials.

As energy affects us we need to experience our emotions, not wallowing in them, but understanding the emotion, freeing ourselves in true awareness. Allow everything to simply be, and observe the beauty and grace with non-attachment. When we are detached, we gain a position of clarity from which we can observe interactions in life instead of being a prisoner of them. In this way we can enjoy every experience and squeeze all the juice from every adventure without judgment. Caring deeply, we act with higher intentions for the betterment of all.

If one can step back from things far enough or view life from the wing of an eagle, the trials of life seem unimportant. In stillness we see the transient nature of life, which teaches us to transcend the battleground and seek the high road.

We all look at things differently. Our minds automatically want to attach qualities like good or bad, useful or useless. How can we make the world a better place if we are standing in the middle of right-and-wrong? Only when we become an observer with non-attachment can we effect change in the world.

Often when we are upset or anxious it is because we identify with something we are attached to. If we focus our attention on what in life we are attached to, we can come to understand we are not that "thing." It is much easier to let go when we no longer identify with things. That is transformation. Let us align with that which resonates Truth and Love.

Isn't life amazing! When we look into the eyes of another we can see, sense, and feel that person's energy. With mindfulness we can watch the trajectory of our own energy and watch the pattern it takes when we interact with others. Observe as your pattern goes up, down, or spirals. When your pattern resonates with an individual or a group your energy is amplified exponentially. When we become an observer with non-attachment and non-judgment we become a soul in wonder.

By developing a creative observational way of seeing we learn a great deal about the nature of the universe and ourselves.

Let us observe our world objectively, free from prejudice or self-interest, so we observe and learn from one another. Being an observer with healthy detachment allows us to know our own hearts with a deeper understanding and appreciation.

Observing balance in nature shows us there is an order present. When we do not observe the world around us, we lose our balance. Our energy is connected to everything, so when we are mindful of that connection we achieve balance. If we work, play, and love connected to our higher consciousness, life is instilled with a greater sense of relaxed spaciousness. Receive life as a gift, and when the time comes, hand it back gratefully.

CHAPTER 40

Purpose

We are always striving for purpose, but unfortunately we rarely allow ourselves to reach a destination. When we live with our True Nature we let go of striving and purpose develops.

Is there a meaning to life? Before addressing that, we should examine whether we are participating in life with conviction and purpose. Do we know who we are and live with spiritual maturity, exemplifying our beliefs? Do we truly understand and work within the power of our loving intentions to co-create our life with Mother Earth as we walk upon her? If we can answer these questions, the answer to "the meaning of life" is clear.

Return to your roots and explore why you are here. Many times it is the coincidences in life that lead us in new directions, and if we examine synchronicity we begin to see a pattern of purpose. Purpose helps us understand that the world we live in is alive with promise. When we realize this we gain a deeper, richer world view that is not based only on survival and comfort. Each of us has a different purpose in life, and at the same time many of us will share a greater purpose. This illustrates our differences and why we have individual gifts to share. It also exemplifies the interconnection of our higher consciousness moving in the direction of a common goal.

As we wander the valleys and canyons of life we help and encourage each other to find our songs. Once we find our melody it takes on a life of its own, rhythmically flowing, joining us together and surprising us.

Wrapped around and interwoven with our loving intentions and commitments is the need to learn about ourselves in depth. Is this life a conscious life, in line with purpose and living in spiritual maturity? The questions we might have about our purpose cannot be answered with our mind; the answers are found in deep listening to our Being, in the sweetness that comes from contemplation. When we understand who and what we are, we begin our exploration with clear vision, which often takes us to places we never imagined or expected on the path to wholeness.

We have many purposes in life yet our soul purpose is all around us, like the colors of a beautiful sunrise, even when we are wandering in the shadows of the valley. Our purpose guides our lives, aligning the necessary experiences and interactions — all we need do is tap in to our Being to witness the higher reality.

Life is a journey of purpose and we live the magic of allowing it to unfold. Be present, participate, and watch the magic.

Find contentment and gratitude in the present moment. This moment of peace allows the Light to fill us with the Divine Potential to carry out our purpose. Joyously move forward with the momentum of loving intention to serve in whatever capacity you choose. Let heart and mind join in clear focus to receive clarity and understanding from our higher selves. When we learn to fully and completely open our hearts to the Divine, then every difficulty and challenge we face and overcome becomes one more achievement in our awakening.

Progressing toward my soul's desire to manifest its life's purpose.

I am in this moment, able to raise my head aloft and face all things free and with love in my heart.

I look to the Light as my friend and companion.

I stand firm and unshaken on my path of purpose.

I steadily fulfill the calling of my awakened life to family, friends, and strangers.

Every moment lived in purpose calls us to join in its unfolding.

We have been entrusted with life and purpose, let us live up to our appointment. We are all subject to Divine Oneness and therein lie the rules of behavior for living virtuously. In this manner we attempt to enjoy the great festival of life. Our purpose draws us to fulfillment and gives us the energy needed to accomplish it. We need only to recall our compassion deep within to know, and allow that knowing to bubble up to our consciousness that we all have a purpose.

Appreciate and spread the joy that is in your heart; investigate the mysteries that cross your path. Let us recall who we are and bring Love to our lives and the planet. Choose to have the Light of Love bring healing to our world. All the wisdom and strength of the Divine is available to us for the asking. Until you light the flame of your Authentic Self, cleansing your Being, there can be no healing. It is the combined purpose of all to find and illuminate our Authentic Self.

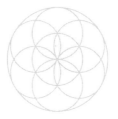

Spirituality ~ Spiritual Maturity

Great and wonderful things need time to grow —first the bud, then comes the flower, and slowly the fruit matures, and the sweetness is available. So it is with spiritual maturity. Once we achieve clear vision we focus on what is truly important, and living life with sweet Love.

On the path to spiritual maturity we realize there is an intelligence that is at the heart of the Universe. We become aware that darkness and Light are held within the same sphere, like Yin and Yang, and they require balance in order to activate being present. We long to know the source of our Being and understand our inner knowing. Seeking insight into the mysteries of life we touch the relation between light, darkness, and us. Mankind has been in a very dark place and now is the time to transition to light. Our path can seem the simplest yet most terrifying of undertakings. The difficult part is getting started, although once you do, it becomes the most natural process. Step out as your Authentic Self, and the Universe will aid and encourage you along the way and across many thresholds. Help the Universe increase your potentials by developing and adding positive life skills. When you learn to drive a car you gain mobility, that skill assists the Universe by increasing your potential to roam further from your home. The same with spiritual maturity: developing your daily practice increases your potentials.

Life is like flowing water, ever-moving and ever-changing. You cannot grasp water without it slipping through your fingers. Water follows the path of least resistance and wears down obstacles in its way. Oh, if we could only flow like water down our true path.

With spiritual maturity we enter a new state of human development. We recognize our higher consciousness as our Divine Nature. Now we awaken to an expanded consciousness in which we are present in the flow of each moment. We experience the interconnection with "All That Is" at this level of consciousness. Yet sometimes we slip out of the flow until we gain the spiritual experience we need to maintain that high level of awareness.

At all stages of development we ask that patience and gentle loving intentions are always present.

Our spiritual experiences are seeds of potential deposited into our radiant Higher Being. Our Higher Being is so much richer than our worldly persona. The act of manifesting even one transformative seed from our Higher Being in our persona will dramatically change us and those around us.

One way to look at spiritual development is as a process of absorbing higher spiritual realities, breaking all the potentials down to see their individual Truths, then reintegrating these distinct fragments into wholeness and unity.

Once you shift to a spiritual perception you ignite the spark of Light within. Once that spark of Light has been struck the heart begins to sing of joy and Love, illuminating a path of inspiration.

Remain true to your Divine Nature by resisting the pull of the material world. Instead honor the spiritual Being in everyone and every thing.

Spirituality is not complicated. The Divine is natural, simple, and efficient. Remember to make time for stillness and rest in the simple calm connection with Spirit to gain clarity of mind. There is no wrong or right way to approach spirituality, as long as you continue to develop your daily practice and bring your contemplations into all of life. As you grow you can draw strength from your practice in challenging times.

Be mindful of your behavior in all situations. Spiritual development depends on mental discipline until it becomes habit. It is a long road that requires balance, and as you progress you are rewarded with colorful experiences. Rise above the temptations of self-inflicted conflicts. Seek the friendship of virtue and truth. Find delight in Being, see the noble goodness, and act with self-mastery.

Our Divine Nature reveals itself as we commit to living a spiritual, heart-centered life. First in small ways, and later in large ways the Divine tells us we are in the stream of conscious awakening, where we are supposed to be, aligned with Universal needs.

Many accomplishments require you, at some point, to give more than you planned. Stay the course. In the end the biggest gain is not the goal but the ability to accomplish.

Each accomplishment builds upon the other, one mindful step at a time leading toward mastery and self-confidence. Within each life are boundless possibilities and potentials, and as we grow our Light continues to evolve. When your spiritual Light touches you, allow it to carry you forward. Allow its unrestrained energy to send you on a quest for wholeness and spiritual maturity. With greater spiritual maturity initiate change with a conscious understanding and mindfulness, without ego, wanting, or fear. We act with the betterment of humanity and Gaia.

We are anxious, confused, and hungry for spiritual growth. Yet, Spirituality does not only exist on some higher plain, and it does not require us to be something other than ourselves. Spiritual Truth lies within, waiting to bubble up like fresh spring water beneath our roots, requiring only that we accept the absolute Truth of Love. Walk with humility and spiritual awareness, with knowledge of the unity and Oneness we share. It is good when we walk together in unity, ascending the staircase of spiritual maturity. Look back from time to time and witness the heights you have gained.

CHAPTER 42

Transformation

*I will play no more — I will recognize when my part is complete
and not lament.*
I will play no more — I will no longer be caught up in grasping.
I will play no more — I will be true to my Divine Self.
I will be grateful for the Love in my life and be empowered.
I will celebrate my liberation!

We easily fall into old habits and hang on to the way things
were, rigid and unyielding. Meanwhile a revolution of change
is knocking on our door. Bend with the movement life is taking and
transform into someone greater. We are shifting from a dominator
world view to one in which we realize life is a precious gift and it is
a privilege to be alive. As we start down the path of transformation
we feel naked and alone, until we experience the connectedness of
the Universe. Seeing ourselves as a part of the whole changes our
perspective forever.

Participate in the transformation of the world. Gaze through the
fog to see clearly what a transformation in consciousness is and promote its development. Examine catalysts and doorways that produce
lifelong and lasting stimulus for transformation. Transformation
happens in our lives as we shift from analytical thinking to an awareness greater than ourselves that is in concert with our minds. Intelligence far greater than the ego begins to operate in our life when we
finally let go of the ego's whispers.

We deserve to become Authentic Beings, true to our higher selves.

Can we as a people change, can we change our behaviors toward love and peace? We know change is inevitable. We can develop a knowing of our fundamental nature, and then we can become adaptive to all environmental changes. In order for transformation to occur we must be fluid, flowing, and flexible. When we are rock solid and unmoving, transformation moves very slowly if at all.

In a flexible flowing state change comes in every moment, allowing purification to filter out the heavy elements, leaving only right action: *~ Flowing Body ~ Flexible Mind ~ Fluid Spirit.*

I AM is me, I AM is you, I AM is us. Together we build a peaceful, flourishing world of respect.

There are so many spiritually transformative experiences in the world trying to give us messages of love and compassion. Yet the messages fall on many deaf ears. A pity, because using the tools of transformation can eliminate so much suffering. Within us is a perfect state of Being, yet our distractions and conscious ignorance pull us away. Plato said, *"If a man neglects education, he walks lame to the end of his life."*

We can overcome and transform into the spirit of Love. Like flowers emerging from the soil we seek the Light. This is our quantum moment — empowering, humbling, and leaving us with a peaceful heart. If we keep focused on our heart's Light it will synthesize the physical and Divine into a coherent whole, propelling us toward understanding. We feel the subtle energy of Love resonate from our heart; we enhance our connectivity by contributing our Love to the global shift.

May our creative Spirit serve us well as we explore the world of unknowing.

We are moving toward greater comprehension of our world as Divine Consciousness feeds us through our desires for understanding the undefined. Let our creative Spirit transform our lives and the lives of those around us in ever expanding circles of loving insight.

To know yourself could not be easier, all you have to do is *Be*. Being present is the catalyst for the transformation we recognize as awakening. Being a soul in wonder allows you to live as yourself without drawing conclusions of what should be. As individuals we submit ourselves to transform into becoming whole. There is no better way to understand the depth of our world and our place in it.

Transformation begins with a spark of Light that nurtures our Being. Contemplation helps us reach within our heart to a doorway that connects us to the infinite Light of our Being. Step into the Light and know your True Being, as a part of the Oneness.

CHAPTER 43

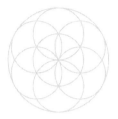

True Being ~ Authentic Being

When we live as an Authentic Being it is like being the Sun in the darkness. Another world is opened in which the darkness is illuminated and the shadows are cast from our vision.

When we begin to accept ourselves and see our True Nature, we begin to walk in the world of Light and Love. Let us begin the journey back to finding our true identity — our True Being. We are not what others think of us. We are not what we do. We — everyone and every thing — are not separate entities. That attitude is our negative ego speaking, developed by our cultural upbringing. Releasing all of that does not have to be difficult. Within each of us is Love's Light, our doorway to Authenticity.

At birth, the first time we are picked up by physical hands, we begin to forget our True Nature. Our shining Being soon gets lost in the mists of physicality and the mind, as we wander through the spiral of life. Yet the link remains, a shimmering cord; a lifeline to our higher self, is waiting for us to pull ourselves out of the haze. This great treasure is protected and hidden carefully within each of us. Why and where it is hidden is for each of us to discover. Through stillness we can go within and contact our Authentic Being and recognize our potential and strengths.

Draw from your deep inner spring of wisdom. Allow your heart to open to your True Being. Step out with a connection to the Divine and know, learn, trust, and share.

Listen to the calm voice within. Understand the source of strength and protection our True Nature carries. Once you connect, the frightening sounds from outside lose their disquieting clamor. Remember to put the emphasis on the heart. Your heart is always one with your True Nature. Discipline your mind to hear the song of your enlightened heart.

Within our inner reality is an illuminated Being; find that the Being is you, that it is your True Nature. Once you recall your essence, you can begin the journey of change. Realize, no matter how wounded or dysfunctional life has been, you can change and return to a contented, happy, radiant Being. When we recognize our True Nature there is no need to look for anything outside ourselves. Desiring more we move away from the knowledge that we are already complete just as we are. Live within your True Nature and you will decrease desire.

Embrace your Authentic Being cleansed of all drama. Work with your connection to Oneness and find the natural buoyant quality of consciousness.

Your Authentic Being gives you a ladder to climb from emotionally blocked states into empowerment and self-mastery. Being in touch with your Authentic Being is your natural state, not some supernatural accomplishment. Deep within we feel the connection to Oneness; we only have to be present to allow that Love in. Acknowledge the Love, bring it into all aspects of life, and abundance and gratitude will be established.

Are you living life as an Authentic Being? Only through integration of inner awareness and balance with our ego can we live authentically. Being authentic means knowing yourself and living with heart-centered intentions. When you feel you are changing or merging with your True Being, you are gratefully balancing ego with spiritual connection. You are developing clear vision to perceive your Being, putting away the masks of false personas once worn. This new vision brings a new knowing: *Being is connected to All, yet can be harmed by none.*

There is no train speeding through the darkness of the past trying to catch you, so do not look back at the shadows of your past. You are awakening to your Authentic Being, on a personal journey of discovery and wonder.

With stillness we see the True Nature of a person, place, or thing, and our consciousness becomes what we are gazing upon.

We get caught up in life's happenings and satisfying our wants, so we forget our essence. Our True Being is beyond form and time, beyond the circumstance that exists within form. Our Authentic Being is limitless. When we develop the daily practice of connection to our Being, we are on the path of conscious awakening and exploring our own development.

When we go deep within we find our essence is truly formless, separate, yet a part of our physical body. Our essence is intensely full and alive with Love for all that is now and will be, flowing with the Source. In contemplation we incorporate many elements that seem unrelated into a healthy whole reality. Connection helps us to discern the reliable, non-judgmental voice of Spirit and the unreliable voice of fantasy and wishful thinking, allowing us to live as Authentic Beings even in a chaotic life.

Be yourself — stop adding unnecessary baggage to who you really are. An Authentic Being does not role-play; an Authentic Being focuses on each moment and experiences it in full. We accomplish more when we do not expend the energy pretending to be something or someone else. *Be* completely you. Let us not define ourselves so we may tap in to our unlimited potential.

CHAPTER 44

Oneness ~ Source ~ Universal All

Explore your separateness and blaze a path that is unique to your abilities. Along the path you will find purpose and Oneness.

The terms Oneness and Source attempt to describe the ineffable. How can we describe the nature of existence and all its harmony? Oneness and Source encompass Universal interconnectedness, which is a multidimensional concept distilled into one-dimensional words. But when spoken with the energy of our heart center, Oneness and Source are capable of opening our consciousness to the vast Divine.

How can we talk about Oneness with those who think they know it yet have not experienced it? How do you describe limitless Light and Love; how do you describe Source? The Oneness is so vast that to describe it labels it, and labeling limits the limitless. Instead we can express our connection through the loving intentions in our hearts, and with our smiles. We can then speak without words getting out of hand. Yes, Oneness is silent, yet peacefully conveys communication. It is infinitely gentle, and yet like a mountain solid and grounded. When touching Oneness all fear disappears and spiritual joy occurs in peaceful silence.

We transcend our physical emotions to a liberation of peace and reside in pure Love, yet we still have our individual identities.

Who are we if we are One? In the Light we experience a merging of our physical bodies with our higher consciousness. As we move through the letting-go process we are reunited with the Light, the Oneness. We find that we are part of the whole, connected to all that is, was, and will ever be. Oneness is knowing, and the ability to be everywhere and in everything, because the Light resides within all things, as well as the spaces between.

Encourage the larger consciousness of Oneness to operate in union with your individual consciousness. Be engaged with the flow as you passively observe it. Just as a river flows and makes its own path, moving rocks and obstacles and diverting the path, we remain amazed at this infinite stream flowing beyond us, and which is not created by us.

Being in harmony with others comes from our experience of unity and thus a way of living life within the flow. It is a natural impulse of our expanded heart to mistakenly take responsibility for the changes in our paths, when all the time it was the flow of Oneness that diverted the path. Become a passive observer in all activities.

ONENESS ~ SOURCE ~ UNIVERSAL ALL

Step out into the world knowing that your essence dwells in the Oneness. The essence of everything in the Universe dwells in the Oneness.

We are capable of communicating with all we experience through Oneness. There are no boundaries; there is no separation or distance with Spirit. The vastness of Oneness is far beyond comprehension, because it is infinite. Yet you can touch this immense Love through Stillness. Go inward and allow yourself to join with Love, knowing you are worthy and deserving to recognize your place within Oneness.

Oneness holds a greater power than anything humanity's pride or arrogance can generate. Love is the unifying power that connects this physical universe to Oneness. When in pain or sorrow focus on the Divine and become a conscious participant in your healing. We all have the Divine within us, giving us the ability to lift ourselves up with Love.

At the core of stillness is the essence of Oneness, leading us to the knowledge that what is most personal and intimate is also universal. Let the vibration of Universal Oneness be a guide in daily activities, helping to manifest a brighter day. The lines of communication are open between this physical world and Oneness, as they have always been and always will be. Take a moment to find them. It is in Love that we ultimately find communication to the Divine and ourselves.

Our whole life is a prayer. Not a prayer you would say in church, but a walking, living prayer of Love and Being.

Looking at our planet's spot within the Universe, this rock with its coating of water is so tiny that it keeps our perspective humble. Yet this rock also has mountains and valleys with grass and forests, birds, animals and humans upon its surface. There are oceans so deep that light cannot penetrate the depths, yet life exists there too, from the smallest microbe to the largest whales. Our spinning blue marble is part of a vast Universe, and as small as it is, it contributes to our ever-expanding cosmos. Isn't it amazing, astounding, and remarkable?

Our connection to a greater Oneness maintains our ego's balance; it keeps us humble and in alignment with our purpose of awakening. We share the purpose of awakening, an essential component of the Universal Whole, with everyone on the planet. Working together we complete each other. Fine-tune your Love; let it resonate and awaken the Divine within. Become one with what life wants, not separate. Release worries and stress, and shine your vibrant Being onto the formless and eternal One. *Be* the walking essence of your divine being.

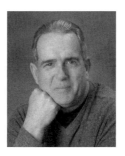

About the Author

David Bennett enjoys the retired life of a public speaker, author, teacher, energetic healer, and transformational life coach. He's had many appearances on radio and television, including on *Dr Oz, Angels Among Us*, NBC national news, and PBS. He publishes articles in numerous magazines, blogs, and papers.

David had three transformative experiences: In 1983 he drowned and had a Near-Death Experience while the Chief Engineer of the ocean research vessel Aloha. He went through a second transformative experience in 1994 when in meditation in Sedona AZ, his childhood home. The third one occurred in November 2000, when he was diagnosed with stage IV lung cancer that metastasized into his spine causing its collapse.

Now in remission and retired/disabled his passion includes volunteering with experiencer groups and cancer survivors to help integrate their spiritually transformative experiences. David works as an energetic healer using a White Light healing technique given to him from Spirit, and as an integration/transformational life coach. He speaks about the transforming events in his life in his book *Voyage of Purpose*, published by Findhorn Press. You can find more about David on his website *DharmaTalks.com* or through social media on Facebook at *DharmaTalk* and Twitter as *DharmaTalks*.

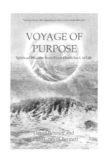

FINDHORN PRESS

Life-Changing Books

Consult our catalogue online
(with secure order facility) on
www.findhornpress.com

For information on the Findhorn Foundation:
www.findhorn.org